Making Math Meaningful®

A Source Book for Teaching Math in Grades One Through Five

By Nettie Fabrie, Wim Gottenbos and Jamie York

Jamie York Press

2016

Making Math Meaningful®

A Source Book for Teaching Math in Grades One Through Five

Text Copyright © 2009 by Nettie Fabrie, Wim Gottenbos and Jamie York

ISBN: 978-1-938210-01-3

All rights reserved. No part of this book
may be reproduced in any form or
by any means, without permission in
writing from the publisher.

Cover Design Copyright © 2003 by Catherine Douglas.

Catherine Douglas was a student at Shining Mountain Waldorf School when she designed the cover to this book. It is an impressive example of how equiangular spirals emerge from nested octagons.

JAMIE YORK
PRESS

*Meaningful Math Books for Waldorf,
Public, Private, and Home Schools*

www.JamieYorkPress.com

Table of Contents

INTRODUCTION 1

THOUGHTS ON TEACHING LOWER GRADES MATH 2

The challenge of teaching math in the lower grades 2
What are the symptoms of our 'math illness'? 2
Principles of Waldorf education 4
Will our children be prepared? 7
In the math classroom 9
The art of teaching math 13
Working with struggling students 18
Golden rules 20

FIRST GRADE MATH 21

SECOND GRADE MATH 30

THIRD GRADE MATH 40

FOURTH GRADE MATH 50

FIFTH GRADE MATH 62

APPENDIX 74

Math curriculum summary for grades one through five 75
A list of games for lower grades math 77
A step-by-step progression for the arithmetic facts 78
Square and triangular numbers 79
Perfect, abundant, and deficient numbers 80
Powers of two table 81
Prime numbers up to 2000 82
Even numbers as the sum of two primes 83
Odd numbers as the difference of two squares 84
Numbers as the sum of two squares 85

−Introduction−

The Math Tightrope
In teaching mathematics, perhaps like no other subject, we find ourselves walking a tightrope. If we step a bit to one side, a sizable portion of the class becomes perplexed and overwhelmed. If we correct ourselves to the other side, the quicker students get bored and the class as a whole doesn't progress enough. For many teachers, each step along this tightrope brings up unpleasant memories from their own childhood.

As Waldorf teachers, we are aware that the teaching of math is more than just an intellectual exercise. We engage the will of the students as we use movement and rhythmical exercises to teach the times tables. Through appropriate stories, we engage the feeling realm of the students and spark their interest in math. Rudolf Steiner, the founder of the first Waldorf school, spoke of the importance of "permeating the soul with mathematics in the right way" and how a healthy relationship to mathematics can benefit the student's later spiritual development.

Certainly, math in a Waldorf school is viewed differently and taught differently. Yet, the problems we face are often the same as in the mainstream. All too often, a class enters middle school with many of the students weak in math and saying, "I'm bad at math, and I hate it."

Why is this so? How can we do better?

About This Book
While this book is intended for someone currently teaching math in a lower grades Waldorf school, the material presented here can be effectively used by any teacher wishing to bring meaningful, age-appropriate math to their students.

Although we have attempted to address many of the issues that we feel are important, we must acknowledge that there is much more to teaching math than what is found within the covers of a book. This book cannot be a substitute – nor can any book – for a proper teacher-training program, where much of the fundamental and necessary philosophy, pedagogical basis, and teaching technique are covered.

There is much good about what is currently happening with the teaching of mathematics in Waldorf schools in North America. This book, perhaps, focuses more on aspects of mathematics teaching that the authors feel are often in need of improvement in Waldorf schools.

A Word of Caution
The authors hope that the contents of this book will be helpful to teachers and bring to consciousness some aspects of math teaching that may otherwise not surface. We hope that this book will generate thought and discussion. This book should not be viewed as a recipe for teaching mathematics in a Waldorf school. Indeed there is no such recipe. This book is merely a resource that reflects the opinions of the authors. There are other opinions as well that may also be called "Waldorf".

The reader (presumably a teacher) should not simply follow instructions or carry out a plan just because it is stated in this book. As always, it is the teacher's job to develop the inner sense of what is right at a particular moment for the class and to create an effective lesson. It is ultimately the teacher's love and creativity that will bring the material alive for the students. No book can give this to the teacher.

Our website
Making Math Meaningful books has a website: **www.JamieYorkPress.com**. On this site, you can view full-color photos of children's main lesson book pages, download (for free!) a variety of practice sheets, and access other resources related to *Making Math Meaningful* books. You can also contact us there with questions and comments.

Our puzzle and game book, and more!
There may be times when the teacher knows it is time to do something different. Our *Making Math Meaningful Puzzle and Game Book* is intended as a resource for math teachers in grades four through twelve, in part to supplement the normal classroom material. It provides ideas for that "something different".

Additionally, we have books for middle school and high school math. Our books can be ordered through our website **www.JamieYorkPress.com**.

Acknowledgements
The authors wish to thank the following people for their help in making this book possible: Marilyn Fox for ideas on second grade place value; Grace Wang, Vienna Scheyer and Katja Kramers, students of the Seattle Waldorf school for sharing their beautiful math main lesson books; Meike Gottenbos for helping with some drawings; and Ruud Luiten for technical support. And a very special thank you goes to Else Gottgens for the many wonderful discussions about child development we have had over the past 35 years.

−Thoughts on Teaching Lower Grades Math−

The challenge of teaching math in the lower grades

Fear and stress

In this day and age, fear can have an influence over much of our lives, including our children's education. Teachers and parents are more worried than ever. "What will happen if my child gets behind?" The pressure to get ahead has increased. Education has become a race! More advanced material at a younger age. More homework. More high stakes testing. More fear. More stress. Even independent schools are affected.

Stress and fear are not conducive to learning anything; they impair our students' ability to learn math. We need to reduce fear and stress and create a calm, safe learning environment, which enables our students to achieve an inner state of calm contemplation. This creates a vessel in which learning math is possible.

Avoiding struggle

Ironically, even though there are greater expectations for our children to learn more material and do more homework – all at a younger age – we don't want them to struggle. We want our children to be happy and successful. We live in an "instant gratification" culture. If we want something to happen, we expect it quickly. And it should be easy. Our children should get A's, be ahead of the others, and be comfortable.

The trouble is that learning math usually isn't that quick and easy. It takes patience – patience for the student, patience for the teacher, and patience for the parents. *Working through struggle is an important part of learning math – and is a great life lesson.* One of our challenges as class teachers today is to create a safe environment – without fear and stress – in which our students can work through their struggles. This is certainly no easy task. Wouldn't it be wonderful if all of our children could learn how to calmly face their challenges and develop confidence as they successfully work through their struggles?

What are the symptoms of our "math illness"?

Meaningless math

What is society's view of math? Math is often not seen as meaningful in and of itself. A widespread belief is that "good math" must be practical and useful. It then follows that the main reason to study math is that it can be useful for some other purpose or subject. All of these attitudes toward math can make it challenging to teach math in a meaningful way.

While we, the authors, believe that practical applications of math can be helpful, we also feel that there is a higher purpose to learning math. (See *Principles of Waldorf Education* below.)

The *LIST*

If people believe that math should always be practical, then it stands to reason that skill development would become the primary focus. Over time this has degenerated into the *LIST* – a horrifically long list of skills that are supposedly necessary for our children to move to the next level (e.g., middle school, high school, or college). The *LIST* manages to put pressure on teachers at all levels of education. They fear that if they don't get through the entire *LIST*, then their students won't be prepared. We are led to believe that this *LIST* is getting longer and longer, and more and more daunting. Such an over-emphasis on skill development is boring or overwhelming (or both) for many students, and for the teacher as well.

We, the authors, believe that basic skills are important, but the list of topics needed to move forward is not horrifically long; it is actually quite manageable (see *What skills are really needed?* below). We also believe there is much more to math than just learning skills. With so much emphasis going toward the mastery of a long list of skills, some of the more interesting aspects of mathematics become neglected. (See *Principles of Waldorf Education* below.)

Making math procedural

The tendency in schools today is to spend far too much time on procedural skills at too young an age. Examples include borrowing in second grade, long division in third grade, and arithmetic with mixed numbers in fourth grade. Each of these topics would probably be better introduced at least a full year later than what was just mentioned. But here's the real issue: by having too much of an emphasis on procedural skills at too young an age, the children experience math as a collection of blind procedures, likely paving the way for math anxiety or trauma. Even for those students who aren't traumatized by the blind procedures, it is likely that they will not

Thoughts on Teaching Lower Grades Math

have an understanding of what they are doing, and that later, in higher grades, they will have troubles when the mathematical concepts become more challenging.

For example, in the process of doing a borrowing problem, such as 72–58, many second or third graders lose sight of the two numbers, 72 and 58. Instead they see columns of numbers: 7 minus 5, and 2 minus 8 (which is made possible through the trick of borrowing). Perhaps worst of all, the young child then loses sight of what subtraction really is; for them subtraction has become this blind procedure called "borrowing".

Likewise, in the process of doing a long division problem, the third or fourth grader forgets that they are doing a division problem; they forget what division really is. And in the process of doing arithmetic with two mixed numbers (e.g., $8\frac{2}{3} + 5\frac{1}{2}$), the fourth grader sees six numbers (8, 2, 3, 5, 1, 2) placed in specific locations. The final answer is then just the end result of a series of steps or tricks. In such cases, much of the work with fractions ends up being a collection of tricks. (See *Be aware of tricks!* below) The student likely forgets that the problem had anything to do with fractions and may not truly understand what a fraction is.

We believe that such procedural skills may be introduced in the lower grades, but that an over-emphasis on these skills when the children are too young often results in the children losing the big picture, not understanding the concepts behind the procedure, and losing (or not developing) their *sense of number*. All of this increases the chance of the child later becoming *math traumatized*.

The big race

Today's society seems to picture education as a race. The names of programs like "No Child Left Behind" and "Head Start" reinforce this image. The impression we are given is that getting ahead early translates into being ahead at the finish. We disagree. Not only is there much more to a child's education than getting ahead, but pushing advanced material on young children (in first through fourth grade) does not translate into being ahead in the long run. In fact, such an approach usually results in (1) "dumbing-down" the material; (2) teaching that is superficial, uninspirational and deadening; and (3) overwhelming many of the students. Instead, the best approach is to proceed slowly in the early grades, ensuring that the material is covered thoroughly, so that all of the students deeply absorb what is being brought to them. Then, after having built such a solid foundation, the children are set to really take off in middle school and high school. The best we can do in the lower grades, if we want our students to be strong when they graduate high school, is to give them a strong foundation in the fundamentals and engender a joy for learning.

Homework[1] and reports

Homework and reports are topics that extend further than the math classroom, but we feel that they are sufficiently important to mention here.

The trend in education today is to give more and more homework at a younger and younger age. Many teachers want to prove to the parents in their class that the children are doing advanced work. Even Waldorf teachers are caving in to this pressure. It's not uncommon today for third graders to be given homework.

We question this trend. We feel that there should be no homework until fifth grade, and, even then, it should be minimal. Any homework should help to create joy in learning. Children spend many hours in school. This is where they should learn to work hard! Children need a life outside school! At home they need to play, read, practice their music instrument, do crafts, draw, paint, do board games[2], take part in the household chores, and spend time with friends and family. To quote Rudolf Steiner:

> *There is another thing to be considered. In the Waldorf School practically all the teaching takes place in the school itself. The burden of homework is lifted, for the children are given very little to do at home. Because all the work is done together with the teachers, the children's attitude is a quite remarkable one.*[3]

It is often said that giving homework in the early grades helps to develop good work habits for later. This gives the impression that the best way to prepare children for the stressful burden of homework, which they will encounter in high school, is to have them experience this burden in the younger grades. In contrast, we feel that good homework habits can be developed in middle school, and even then, with a minimal amount of homework.

In a similar way, teachers now require the children to do written reports (e.g., animal reports in fourth grade, state reports in fifth grade, and book reports). It seems that this comes from mainstream education where there is a desire to imitate an aspect of higher-level education (i.e., research papers). It gets watered down and

---

[1] For further reading that questions the value of homework, see Alfie Kohn's book, *The Homework Myth*.
[2] See the appendix for a list of games for lower school math.
[3] *Human Values in Education*, The Teachers' Conference in the Waldorf School, Lecture V, Arnheim, July 21, 1924.

brought to the young children. Parents who are pushing for more academics may be pacified. But we feel that such reports have little pedagogical value and can even have a negative impact on the child's enthusiasm for learning. We have similar concerns about book reports. Of course, there is nothing wrong with encouraging children to read a book at home. But forcing children to read a book that they may not be interested in, and then burdening them with writing a report on it, is likely to dampen their enthusiasm for reading.

Math trauma

Many adults in our society are weak in math and intimidated by it. Why does this happen? At what age did the math trauma begin? At what age does a child start saying, "I'm bad at math"? While for some students math trauma may not be apparent until adolescence, we believe that in most cases the root causes of math trauma begin between second and fourth grade.[4]

Perhaps our single greatest task when teaching math in the lower grades is to ensure that our students don't enter middle school math traumatized. But this is no easy task!

Two ends of the spectrum

<u>Too much too soon</u>. Class teachers can be pressured by parents or colleagues to prove that their own class is strong at math, doing advanced material, and ahead (or at least not behind) other classes. The teacher may or may not be conscious of this pressure, and much of this pressure may be self-inflicted. Because of this pressure, the teacher is then inclined to move quickly through the material and go into too much depth with material when the students are too young. All of this will likely lose a good portion of the class, leaving them math traumatized and thinking that they will never become good at math. Such a class often enters middle school with a huge disparity between those who are good at math (the "fast students") and those who aren't good at math (the "slow students"), with few students in between. (See *Avoiding the "Great Divide"* below.)

<u>Math deprivation</u>. Don't mistake what has been said above as an argument to do as little math as possible. If a teacher avoids math because he or the students find it unpleasant, or the teacher keeps the math too simple, then the class won't progress enough, and the students' sense of number and ability to "think mathematically" will be underdeveloped. Such students will likely have difficulties in later years when they have a teacher who has higher expectations.

It's all about balance. We need to have (reasonably) high expectations of our students. Each student should be appropriately challenged in math. Developing a sense for what is right for the class is an important part of the art of teaching.

Lack of independent, creative and flexible thinking

Certainly one of the ultimate goals of any educational system should be that its graduates can think independently, flexibly, and creatively. Yet, we often hear from university professors and leaders in industry that today's education isn't able to adequately produce graduates who are good problem-solvers and can think creatively. Clearly, an approach to teaching math that amounts to marching through a textbook and blindly memorizing procedures is not likely to develop independent thinking.

Students are often given the impression that there is only one way to do a math problem – that math is rigid and inflexible. We need to instead look for opportunities to show that there are multiple ways to solve a problem, and elicit from our students their different ideas for doing a calculation or solving a problem. If we are successful with this in the younger grades, it can make it possible for our students to develop into independent and creative thinkers in high school and beyond. (See also *Developing flexibility in thinking* below.)

Principles of Waldorf Education

Waldorf education's principles and unique goals are drawn from the developmental insights of Rudolf Steiner. What is listed here is an essential part of any Waldorf teacher-training program for class teachers. Some of these most important principles are as follows:

<u>Child development</u>. It is important that all Waldorf teachers (from pre-K to grade 12) have a deep understanding of child development and the development of the human being in general.

<u>Developmentally appropriate material</u>. With this understanding of child development, the teacher can then become conscious of how something brought into the classroom affects the children developmentally. A central principle of Waldorf education is that the curriculum supports the development of the child. The right subject at

---

[4] McLeod, DB, (1992). *Research on affect in mathematics education: A reconceptualization*. From Grouws (Ed.), *Handbook of research on mathematics teaching and learning* (pp. 575–596). New York: Macmillan.

the right time does this. For example, in fourth grade, as the child separates from the world, the unity of his surroundings falls apart. Therefore, at this time in the curriculum, we see this reflected in the introduction to fractions, where the whole number falls into many pieces. This process with fractions helps to support the child through this transition in his life.

Working with the imagination. It is important for the teacher to work with enlivening images and pictures through the children's imaginations rather than using dead concepts and judgments.

Teaching from the whole to the part. By proceeding from the whole to the parts, we divide or restructure the whole into multiple parts. For example, imagine that we have 12 chestnuts and we ask the students to divide these chestnuts. There are many possibilities for dividing the whole of 12 into parts.[5] If we go from the parts to the whole (e.g., and ask, "What is 10 + 2?") we have only one possible answer. This is a materialistic gesture. If we instead go from the whole to the parts, we have a more social gesture – a "giving-away" gesture.

The conscious use of forgetting.[6] One might think that if we were successful in teaching the children, they would then always remember what they were taught; if they forget what they were taught, then it must be a sign that we have failed. But this is not so. *Forgetting is an important part of learning.* After teaching something new to the children, we should then let it go. It "goes to sleep" in the children and works on them subconsciously. Then, after some time, we review – bringing the old topic back and deepening it. The children will have forgotten what they had previously known, but then, during this review process, they will quickly remember it all, and have a new, deeper understanding of the material.

The pedagogical law.[7] As a central tenet of Waldorf education, the teacher educates each of the student's (finer) bodies by working out of his[8] higher body. In kindergarten and early childhood education, the young child is largely working on the development of his physical body. Therefore, the teacher works out of his etheric body while working with imitation. Prior to the teenage years, it is the teacher's astral body that aids the development of the student's etheric. After that, it is the teacher's ego that helps to develop a healthy astral body in the students.

Educating the "freed etheric body"

During the child's first seven years, the etheric forces were used to shape the physical body. With the change of teeth, some of these forces are then freed up and available for the learning process. The education of this freed etheric in the child starts in first grade. What has been developed unconsciously in the first seven years will come to blossom in the next seven years through our work in the classroom. After age seven we can begin to work with the freed etheric forces and nourish the astral body. What we are trying to cultivate is memory, lasting habits, temperaments, lasting inclinations, and enduring desires.[9] [10]

Let's be clear what we mean when we say we need to work on the child's etheric body. When most Waldorf teachers think of working with the children's etheric bodies, they tend to think mostly of *rhythm*. The teachers then tend to spend more time and energy with the rhythmical activities in the lesson than working to strengthen the memory forces.[11] Every morning in a Waldorf school, we can hear many rhythmical activities, mainly done by the teacher, where the whole class follows at will. In these cases, the children often don't work enough individually with the material.

However, working with the child's freed etheric body actually has more to do with *memory, habits and imagination*. "Fully conscious repetition cultivates the true will's impulse."[12] Instead of just counting the beats by ones every day, the teacher should also work with the students counting the windows, the eyes, the noses, the fingers, the legs of the chairs, etc. "A more unconscious repetition cultivates feeling."[13]

---

[5] Rudolf Steiner, *Renewal of Education by R Steiner*, Chapter 10 (Synthesis and Analysis in Human Nature and Education) Lecture given in Basel, May 5, 1920.

[6] Rudolf Steiner, *The Being of Man and His Future Evolution: Forgetting.* Lecture given in Berlin, November 2, 1908

[7] Rudolf Steiner, *The Education of the Child in the Light of Anthroposophy*, 1907. Discusses the birth of the human being's four bodies. These lectures were given eleven years before the start of the first Waldorf School.

[8] Throughout this book, we shall use the words "him" and "he" in the generic sense, as opposed to "he/she" and "him/her". This is done in order to make things more readable.

[9] Rudolf Steiner, *The Etheric Being in the Physical Human Being.* Lecture in Berlin, April 20, 1915 GA 157.

[10] J. Bockemuehl, et.al., *Towards a Phenomenology of the Etheric World.* (pp 217-235).

[11] Rudolf Steiner, *Memory Persephone, Education and Teaching as Preventative Medicine.* Excerpts from Chapter 6. Published by the Medical Section, Dornach, Switzerland, 2006.

[12] Rudolf Steiner, *Study of Man.* Stuttgart, August 21-September 5, 1919, Chapter 4.

[13] Rudolf Steiner, *Study of Man.* Stuttgart, August 21-September 5, 1919, Chapter 4.

Thoughts on Teaching Lower Grades Math

Review and Practice

In Waldorf pedagogy, the word "review" is used in two ways: (1) daily review, which helps the child recall what was done during the previous day's lesson, and (2) review of material that was covered some time ago. Both are an important part of the learning process. Unfortunately, both are often skipped or done ineffectively, even in our Waldorf schools.

Regarding the first meaning of the word "review", Rudolf Steiner emphasized in his book, *The Study of Man*, the importance of how the teacher must be conscious of using the child's sleep life as part of the learning process. This is a central tenet of Waldorf pedagogy. Therefore the teacher must review – bring it back into the child's imagination – the new material from the previous day. In doing this, the teacher should review the lesson from the previous day by using different examples. For instance, in first grade, we might regroup 12 children, and then the next day during the review we might regroup 12 chairs. Then we can go further by working with a new number.

The second meaning of the word "review" relates to the word "practice"; the children should practice material from the current block (when the class is in a math block), previous blocks, and previous grades. In today's culture, there seems to be less patience for review and practice. Teachers today are often hesitant to have their students practice very much because they feel that it isn't interesting for the students. In contrast, we believe that review and practice are vitally important for successful math lessons. However, keep in mind that it may be best to allow new material that has just been introduced in one block to "sleep" until the next math block. This new material is not mentioned again until the next math block, at which point it is reviewed and practiced. Once that math block has been concluded (and the class is in a non-math block), this material (from two blocks ago) can then be occasionally worked into the daily 10 minutes of math practice time.

Students can only learn math skills through adequate and systematic review and practice. The teacher needs to ensure that the students review and practice both the new material and topics covered in previous blocks. An old teacher's motto states that for a student to learn something permanently it should be reviewed the next day, the next week, the next month, and the next year. That is systematic review!

However, be sure that there is joy during math practice time. The problems should be interesting; there should always be something new to discover.

Teaching economically

In a Waldorf school, we are able to teach fewer hours of math than what is done in the mainstream, and still our students do fine and usually are ahead of students from other schools. We teach economically! This is possible for a number of reasons. First of all, the Waldorf class teacher stays with the class for several years, which enables the teacher to develop a deeper relationship with their students and to better know the students' strengths, weaknesses, and how they learn. In a Waldorf school, we are doing much more than teaching skills. We develop capacities in our students. Starting in the early grades, we work on developing the students' observation skills, which allows them to more easily relate one situation to another, and thereby more easily solve a new math problem. These are just some of the reasons that Waldorf education stands out!

A higher purpose

Rudolf Steiner spoke about how mathematics is a training in sense-free thinking. He also spoke about how the proper teaching of mathematics is an important part of the students' moral and spiritual development. By developing mathematical capacities in our students, we are helping to lay the foundation for the students' spiritual development later in life.

> "The student of mathematics must get rid of all arbitrary thinking and follow purely the demands of thought. In thinking in this way, the laws of the spiritual world flow into him. This regulated thinking leads to the most spiritual truths." -- Rudolf Steiner[14]

The Waldorf class teacher

All teachers have a tremendous responsibility to oversee the development of the children in their class. Additionally, all Waldorf teachers have a great deal of freedom in deciding what to bring into the classroom. They do not rely on textbooks; instead each child creates his own book for every main lesson.[15]

---

[14] Rudolf Steiner, *Spiritual Ground of Education,* lecture given at Oxford, August 21 1922, GA 305

[15] A *main lesson* in a Waldorf school takes place first thing in the morning for about two hours. A variety of activities might be done during this time, but the subject of the main lesson changes every four weeks or so.

Thoughts on Teaching Lower Grades Math

It is important that we, as Waldorf teachers, are the authors of what comes into the classroom. It needs to be clear to us why we do what we do. We shouldn't just blindly do something because it's what everyone else does. We need to feel it's right for the students in front of us. In this way we take ownership of the curriculum.

Faculty study

As a faculty, we need to study Anthroposophy. The teaching of mathematics is one of the instruments that we use to aid the children in their development. Studying child development (e.g., temperaments, polarities and the senses) gives us a deeper understanding of the children and helps inspire us in our math lessons. This is an essential part of being a Waldorf teacher.

Imagination and math

In today's society, imagination is associated largely with fantasy and not viewed as very "useful". It is therefore not surprising that in mainstream education, the development of the child's imagination can be considered unimportant. In contrast, Waldorf education holds that the development of the child's imagination is a central aspect of developing the whole child.

Until the age of 13 or 14, the child thinks mainly in pictures and images. If we want these younger children to work willingly, images will motivate them. If we want them to learn eagerly, then pictures will entice them to listen and remember. When we prepare our lessons, we should ask ourselves: "Have I found the proper images for what I want them to learn?"[16]

In terms of the teaching of math, imagination can be woven into the lessons, not just by telling compelling stories, but also by showing students that math is a fascinating and creative human endeavor. In this way, math can be a springboard for thinking flexibly and creatively.

> "Imagination is more important than knowledge. Knowledge is limited. Imagination encircles the world." -- Albert Einstein

Will our children be prepared?

Preparation for middle school, high school and college math

Often we hear parents who worry about their children's math, say: "Will our children be prepared?" This certainly is a fair question. We may then ask, "Prepared for what?" Usually the anxiety is regarding preparation for the next step – whether this next step is middle school, high school, or college. And today, this anxiety about "being prepared" seems to be with children at a younger and younger age.

It is an interesting exercise to ask a group of parents who have this question – and perhaps the anxiety as well – what they think it would look like to have their children well prepared in math for the "next step". Surprisingly, when brought in this way, parents won't usually speak of the necessity for their child to learn a long list of math skills, nor will they say how important it is that their child be ahead of other students.

We believe that there are four critical ingredients that our children need in order to be prepared for their next step in their math education – be it middle school, high school, or college.

1. *Enthusiasm for learning.* Enthusiasm and love for learning math will likely take any student a long way. No matter how good their skills are, no parent or teacher wants their child to be apathetic about learning.
2. *Study skills.* The term "study skills" is broad; it includes organization, work habits, etc. In the lower grades, we prepare and plant the seeds for the work in the higher grades by developing good habits, which includes ensuring that the students complete their work, that their work is well organized, readable, and that they show interest and take pride in their work. Along these lines, we should ask: "Have they learned how to learn, and do they have confidence in their abilities to learn new material?"
3. *Higher level thinking.* All too often in today's world, students graduate from high school and college unable to think for themselves. Their thinking, even when doing math, is largely imitative; they can do math problems as long as they have seen something similar before. As Waldorf educators, our goal is to have students graduate high school who can think flexibly, creatively, and independently. We want our students to be able to think for themselves, think analytically, and we hope that their thinking is heart-felt and imbued with imagination. Once again, this starts in the lower grades. If we don't start here, it is unlikely that we will reach this goal in the upper grades.

---

[16] Else Gottgens, *Waldorf Education in Practice*.

Thoughts on Teaching Lower Grades Math

4. *Basic math skills.* Yes, skills are important. If the students don't master the basic skills, they will not feel confident in moving forward. However, the list of necessary skills needed for the next step isn't as daunting as we might be led to believe...

What math skills are really needed?

Math educators often agree that there is too much of an emphasis on procedural skills in math education today. They say that we need to find more time to develop problem-solving skills (something that begins in the lower grades, but becomes more important later) and creative thinking capabilities. Yet, many teachers complain that there is never enough time for these "extras". We can begin to feel that there is an overwhelming amount of material that the students must learn, and, if they don't learn it all, they won't be ready for the next step. As we stated above, the actual list of necessary skills is relatively short. The below lists are simply intended as benchmarks in two-year intervals.

Skills needed by the end of fourth grade

1. Arithmetic facts learned "by heart". By the end of third grade, the students should know all of the arithmetic facts (including addition, subtraction, multiplication and division) by heart. Work in fourth grade simply reinforces what they learned earlier. (See *Learning Arithmetic Facts by Heart* below.)
2. Sense of Number. Teaching the children so that they develop a "sense of number" is very important, but is not something that comes easily or can be taught directly. (See *Developing a Sense of Number* below)

What about the rest of the skills? Our answer to this question may appear either shocking or pleasantly surprising. Procedural skills do not need to be mastered before fifth grade. The key word here is "mastered". Of course, the students should be introduced to many of these procedural skills before fifth grade. (See also *Making math procedural* above.)

Skills needed by the end of sixth grade

Note: many of the below-mentioned skills may have been introduced earlier, but should be mastered (after a brief review) by the end of sixth grade.

1. The four processes. This includes vertical arithmetic (i.e., carrying, borrowing, long multiplication, and long division), which was no doubt introduced in the early grades, but may not be fully mastered until fifth grade by most students. For more complicated problems, some students may not achieve full mastery until the end of sixth grade.
2. Fractions and decimals. Fractions are introduced in fourth grade, but thorough practice of fraction skills only starts in fifth grade. It will take much of sixth grade before many students will be completely comfortable with fractions. Decimals (i.e., "decimal fractions") should be a fairly easy step if the groundwork with fractions has been laid adequately.
3. Measurement. Measurement is introduced in third grade as a main lesson, reviewed and practiced in fourth grade, and then the metric system is introduced in fifth grade. The students should have mastery over simple conversion problems in both the U.S. system (e.g., How many ounces is 3 pounds?) and the metric system (e.g., How many meters is 5.8cm?). Estimating measurement is also an important skill to be learned.
4. Estimation. For example, estimating that 573×42 is approximately 24,000.

Skills needed by the end of eighth grade

Note: many of the below-mentioned skills may have been introduced earlier, but should be mastered (after a brief review) by the end of eighth grade.

1. Percents. Percents should be briefly introduced in sixth grade, reviewed and furthered in seventh grade (but still kept quite simple!), and then really developed and solidified in eighth grade.
2. Ratios and proportions. Ratios and proportions are an important theme in seventh and eighth grade math.
3. Basic algebra. This includes signed numbers, formulas, and basic equations (e.g., $8 - x + 3 = 2x - 7 - 9x$).
4. Measurement. This includes basic problems with area (e.g., of a circle) and volume (e.g., of a cube).
5. Dimensional analysis. This mostly consists of conversions between the U.S. and the metric system (e.g., 5.2cm is how many inches?). Students should be able to use a conversion table to help with these calculations.

The major themes for math

Grades 1-4: Developing a sense of number

These early grades are not about the mastery of written procedural skills (e.g., vertical arithmetic and calculations with fractions), even though these procedures were introduced in grades three and four. First through fourth grade is about developing a sense of number. Written procedural skills can be firmed up starting in fifth grade.

Grades 5-6: Consolidating skills

In fifth and sixth grade, we consolidate skills that were introduced in earlier grades and develop mastery with written procedural skills, such as doing arithmetic problems in vertical form (i.e., carrying, borrowing, long multiplication, and long division) and doing arithmetic with fractions. Sixth grade is also about seeing the interconnectedness in math (e.g., the relationship between fractions, decimals, percents and division).

Grades 7-9: Developing abstract thinking

This is also the time to develop the students' confidence in their own thinking. Seventh grade is the "eye of the needle" – it is often then that the student's relationship to math is determined for high school and beyond.

Grades 10-12: Developing logical, analytical, synthetic thinking

If all of the groundwork has been properly laid, then this is when we truly see the fruits of all the earlier hard work that has been put into the child's education. Academics, "real math", and independent thinking can all really take off at the end of high school as the student begins to find his own identity and destiny.

Preparation for life

Of course, there is much more to education than preparing our students for math in middle school, high school, or college. Patrick Bassett, former head of NAIS (National Association of Independent Schools), asks the question: "What skills and values are necessary for students to succeed and prosper in the 21st century?"[17]

In order to answer this question, Bassett refers to several sources, including: a Harvard-based study; the government's commission on education; a think tank for higher education; the academic testing industry; public opinion surveys; Tony Wagner's *Seven Survival Skills*; and Howard Gardner's book, *Five Minds for the Future*. What Bassett finds is a surprisingly high degree of congruence between these very different sources.

In the end, Bassett's own list of skills and values needed for the 21st century is:

1. *Character.* This includes qualities, such as self-discipline, empathy, integrity, resilience, courage, etc.
2. *Creativity.* It goes without saying that a strength of an arts-integrated curriculum is developing creativity in its students. But it is also important that our education helps to develop creative thinking as well. Later in life, this quality manifests itself as adaptability and developing an entrepreneurial spirit.
3. *Critical thinking.* This includes problem solving, the ability to analyze information (filtering, analysis, and synthesis), questioning what you are "told" in the media, and thinking for yourself.
4. *Communication.* This is more than just reading and writing. Bassett is very clear that the emphasis here is public speaking. Yet, in today's information world of media and computer screens, children (and adults!) are losing their abilities to speak articulately. Think of how beneficial it is to have the students, year after year, stand in front of an audience and speak – be it in a dramatic play, or at an all-school assembly.
5. *Teaming.* The ability for people to work together productively and collaboratively has become more important than ever. And today's youth loves working in groups!
6. *Leadership.* Today, perhaps more than ever, the world is in need of inspirational leaders, who have strong values, and the courage and will to "stand up for the good".

We believe that the above six skills and values speak for the strength (and need!) of Waldorf education.

In the math classroom

Two types of topics: Skills and Mathematical Experiences

As teachers, it is only natural that our own education deeply influences our view of mathematics. For most of us, our formal math education worked largely like this: the teacher explained a new concept; the teacher gave us examples of solving problems with this new topic; we practiced the new problems for homework; after some time, we were tested; and, at some point later, the topic was reviewed. In spite of much work on teaching

---

[17] Patrick Bassett, *Demonstrations of Learning for 21st Century Schools*, Independent Perspective (Journal), Fall 2009.

methods in mathematics, and many experiments with mathematics curriculum, this model for teaching math remains prevalent today from elementary school to graduate school. In many cases this model for teaching math is both appropriate and effective; in many cases it is not.

This method for teaching math is completely focused on skills. It probably is most useful in grades seven through nine. In earlier years, such a skills-based approach should be used sparingly. In later years (upper high school and beyond), students should be encouraged to think more on their own and not just imitate their teacher.

As teachers, we sometimes think that the students are supposed to "learn" everything that we teach – that everything should be learned, tested, and retained. However, that's not true. It can be helpful to consider that math topics can be divided into two categories: *skills* (i.e., material that needs to be mastered) and *mathematical experiences*.

Skills (a topic that needs to be mastered). Here the teacher needs to create a dance between introducing, deepening, practicing, sleeping, and reviewing. The bigger the topic (e.g., fractions), the greater the number of times it needs to be put to sleep, and then later reviewed. It is quite typical to introduce a skills topic one year, but not to have the students reach mastery until the next year, or the year after.

Mathematical experiences. With a "pure" mathematical experience, there is often no expectation that the students remember the topic or learn it as a skill. Examples of such topics include puzzle problems, "Wonder of Number" topics, number bases (8th grade), and a variety of geometric topics. We teach these topics because they stretch our students' minds, teaching them to think mathematically, and they engender enthusiasm and wonder for math.

And, of course, we should acknowledge that many topics can be considered a mix of skills and mathematical experiences.

Learning the arithmetic facts[18]

Far too often, students going into sixth grade are too slow with arithmetical procedures (e.g., long division, multiplication) simply because they don't know their arithmetic facts. This should not happen.

Knowing the arithmetic facts has nothing to do with how "smart" a student is. In reality, a lack of confidence often causes students to do poorly in math during their middle school and high school years. This lack of confidence often starts from them not knowing their multiplication facts, which makes them *think* that they must be bad at math, and in the end it can turn into a self-fulfilling prophecy.

There is a fairly narrow window – the center of which is third grade – for learning the arithmetic facts. It is much more difficult to learn these facts by heart after fourth grade.

So how can we reach our goal of having all of our students learn their arithmetic facts by heart by the end of third grade? The real key to achieving this goal is working systematically and creatively with the children starting in first grade. Also, to help in this effort, we have prepared *arithmetic facts practice sheets* that can be used in third grade, and have also prepared practice sheets for review and increasing speed for fourth and fifth graders. These sheets can be downloaded for free from our website: **www.JamieYorkPress.com**.

For more details, be sure to read the following two sections of this book:
- *A Step-by-step Progression for the Arithmetic Facts* (in the appendix).
- *All about the Third Grade Arithmetic Facts Practice Sheets* (under *More Ideas for Teaching Third Grade Math*).

Word problems

At times, word problems are held up as being more important than they really are. Some say that word problems show how math can be useful in the real world, and that word problems help to develop problem-solving abilities. Neither is necessarily true. In truth, many students (especially in the upper grades) quickly learn to hate word problems; they shut down as soon as they see a word problem.

There are many different types of word problems, and many levels. It is helpful to keep in mind that the analytical thinking abilities needed for true problem solving only really blossom toward the end of high school.

Our point here is not to say that word problems should be avoided until high school. Word problems should be brought into the classroom, starting in first grade, through stories and images. But we should be very careful! We need to keep in mind the pedagogical purpose of word problems. Word problems can help students see the interconnectedness of language – how English can be used to express a math problem. Word problems – if well

---

[18] Throughout this book, the term "arithmetic facts" refers to all of the basic facts that should be learned by heart, including the addition facts (up to 18=9+9), the corresponding subtraction facts, the multiplication facts up to the 12's table (of course, out of order), and the corresponding division facts.

chosen – can show how mathematics can appear in our everyday lives. We need to carefully consider how to bring word problems to the class in a way that isn't traumatizing. Keep it simple, and make it fun!

Mental arithmetic[19]

In our modern technological world, it may seem that the ability to work with numbers in your head is no longer necessary. We strongly disagree. Mental arithmetic is an important skill to be developed from first grade up through middle school. If practiced regularly in the classroom, mental arithmetic strengthens the students' sense of number, challenges their memory, increases their ability to focus, and develops general cognitive capacities. The use of calculators weakens the students' ability to do mental arithmetic. We therefore discourage the use of calculators before eighth grade.

Mental arithmetic can be worked on in a variety of ways, including orally with the whole class, or individually on paper (e.g., arithmetic facts practice sheets). It can be used for practicing skills (arithmetic facts in third or fourth grade, or simple fraction practice in fifth grade), or it can focus more on simply developing the ability to work with numbers in your head. As a guideline, mental arithmetic should be practiced daily for 10 minutes or less. Examples of mental arithmetic calculations are:

- Arithmetic facts. Before fourth grade, much of mental arithmetic may consist of practicing the basic arithmetic facts.
- Number journeys. For example, what is 5 plus 8, minus 3, times 6, divided by 2, divided by 5? Be careful though – weaker students may give up on number journeys.
- "Halfway" problems. These can be done for different grade levels. For example, in second grade, you could ask: "What is halfway between 3 and 9?" In fifth grade: "What is halfway between 423 and 428?"
- Counting backwards. This is very helpful in the early grades. But even for fourth or fifth graders it can be helpful to ask the students to state the five numbers coming before a particularly large number (e.g., 3780).
- Remembering large numbers. This is good especially for fourth grade and up. Take a problem that everyone could easily do on paper, and have them do it in their head. This requires great concentration and memory. Examples: 78+28; 234+38; 612–67.
- Subtracting from 100, 1000, etc. This is good practice starting in third grade.
  Examples: 100–35; 100–72; 600–32; 1000–222; 500–374; 1,000,000–36.
- Mental arithmetic "shortcuts". In our sixth and seventh grade workbooks, there are 27 calculation shortcuts (referred to as "math tricks"). Some of the simple ones can be done in fourth and fifth grade. Examples: 300 x 5, 30 x 50, and 4.82 x 10. It is important, however, that there is a process through which the class was guided that brings the students to an understanding of why the trick works. (See *Be aware of tricks!* under *The art of teaching math* below.)

A word of caution. As with word problems, there is a tendency for some students to give up with mental arithmetic. So the same rules apply: keep it simple, and make it fun! However, it can be best to challenge the students with a tough problem at the end.

Developing a "Sense of Number"

Having the students develop a sense of number is an important goal for lower grades math. However, this is very challenging.

It seems that some students were born with a natural sense of number. And for other students it seems as if they will never develop a real sense of number or be able to think mathematically. Yet, often, if we allow the curriculum to soak in, and allow the student to slowly move along with their math work – all the while being patient and not anxious – then one day (maybe in fourth or fifth grade) we are pleasantly surprised to see that this student has indeed been able to develop a modest sense of number and a healthy relationship to math.

Certainly, some of what we do with our math lessons (e.g., mental arithmetic) directly helps develop the children's sense of number. Yet, just as importantly, and less well understood, is what should be avoided. What follows is an incomplete list of things that can help develop the students' sense of number:

- Do daily mental arithmetic. Beginning in second grade, this may be the best way to directly improve the students' sense of number. (Also see *mental arithmetic* above.)
- Number dictations. Learning to read and write numbers up into the millions helps the child to develop a sense of number.

---

[19] By "mental arithmetic", we are referring to doing calculations in your head without writing down your work.

Thoughts on Teaching Lower Grades Math

- <u>Estimating</u>. Starting in first grade with estimating the number of apples in a basket, or the number of people in a room, continuing with larger estimations in second grade, estimating measurement starting in third grade, and estimating the answers to difficult vertical arithmetic problems – estimating is a great way to strengthen the students' sense of number. There are endless possibilities for bringing estimation into the classroom!
- <u>Don't force the memorization of the arithmetic facts too early</u>. Often parents and teachers become nervous when they see children using their fingers to do calculations. The real question here is: at what age is counting on your fingers acceptable, and when should a student no longer be doing this? We feel that in second and third grade (and perhaps even into fourth grade for some students) using fingers to calculate can be positive; this can mean that the child is thinking through the problem, which in general is good for developing a sense of number. If the child were to memorize his arithmetic facts in second grade, then that child would miss out on the benefits of "figuring it out yourself" (e.g., instead of memorizing 8+5 = 13, he thinks, "from 8, I go up by 2 to get to 10, then another 3 to get to 13"). That can do wonders for developing a sense of number!
- <u>Allow for different methods</u>. By showing different methods to do calculations, students learn to be flexible and creative in their thinking, which can then help to develop a sense of number. Of course, there needs to be balance. If we always show just one method to solve a problem, then the students can become inflexible in their thinking. At the other extreme, showing different methods to solve almost every problem can confuse and overwhelm many students. (See also *Developing Flexibility in Thinking* below.)
- <u>Keep in the horizontal as much as possible</u>. We believe that this is very important. Far too often, students are trained at too young an age to write all arithmetic problems in vertical form. Therefore, 73–65, and 65+18 are both written vertically. Instead of *thinking* about the two given numbers and trying to figure out what the answer is – which, of course, helps to develop a sense of number – the problem just becomes a carrying or a borrowing problem, and the student is instead just working with columns of numbers. Therefore, we recommend that carrying and borrowing *not* be introduced until third grade. Even after carrying and borrowing have been introduced, it is important to have the students continue doing arithmetic both in the horizontal form (with practice sheets) and orally with mental arithmetic.
- <u>Minimize blind procedures</u>. Related to what has just been said above…in general, procedures where the children follow steps blindly inhibit the development of a sense of number. This does not mean that such procedures (e.g., borrowing, long division, arithmetic with fractions, etc.) should be done at all. But it may be a reason to delay the introduction of such procedures, and even after a procedure has been introduced, we should be careful to not overemphasize it. We need to be sure that the students still maintain their ability to do calculations the "old way" (i.e., horizontal arithmetic and mental arithmetic). (See also *Making Math Procedural* above.)
- <u>When in doubt, wait</u>! In general, when the students are introduced to a topic before they are developmentally ready, then they will tend to simply follow the procedure without really understanding what they are doing. We should *not* be asking: "How soon can I get the children to learn this topic?", but rather: "Are the children developmentally ready to receive this topic?"
- <u>Allow for discovery</u>. There are many times when it is completely appropriate for the teacher to show the class how to do something in math and then have the children practice it. However, it is important to look for opportunities for the students to discover things on their own. By discovering things on their own, students become excited about learning and the material becomes more meaningful. It also helps to develop flexibility in their thinking and helps to develop their sense of number. Examples include:
  - With addition and multiplication (around second grade), knowing that the terms can be reversed and the result will be the same. (E.g., 6x10 is the same as 10x6.)
  - When multiplying with zeroes (around fourth grade), knowing that zeroes can be ignored and then added back later. (E.g., 40x70, 400x7, and 4x700 are all equal to 2800.)
  - When subtracting two large numbers (starting around second grade), we can add instead subtract to get the answer. (E.g., with 73–68, we can think of it as taking 2 steps from 68 to 70, and then 3 steps from 70 up to 73. Our answer is then 2+3, which equals 5.)
  - When dealing with cost problems (around fifth grade), we can first determine the unit cost of one item and then use this to determine the price of a certain number of that item. (E.g., if oranges are being sold at a rate of 5 for 75¢, then we first calculate that the unit cost is 15¢ per orange, so 8 oranges would cost 15x8, which is $1.20.)

The art of teaching math

The three myths of math

Myth #1. *Only people born with math ability can become good at math.* In reality, hard work can help develop math ability. In such cases, a student in the upper grades who is seen as being strong in math, might very well have once struggled with math. On the other hand, it can happen that a student, who had strong math ability and never worked at it, ends up quite weak at math.

Myth #2. *Confusion is bad.* In reality, confusion is part of learning math. Every time we learn a new topic in math, we must go through a period of confusion as we gain clarity. A key difference between a student who is strong at math versus a student who struggles is that the strong student is usually completely comfortable with working through this period of confusion as they come to clarity, whereas the struggling student often gets frustrated and shuts down. (See also *Working with Struggling Students* below.)

Myth #3. *Forgetting is bad.* In reality, forgetting is an important part of learning. As teachers, we can sometimes think (perhaps subconsciously) that if we have taught something well, then the students will learn it and won't ever forget it. In Waldorf education, we believe it is important to work with the students sleep life. It is good and normal for the students to forget something that they have been taught. And if it is something that we want the students to learn permanently, then we need to review it. In fact, for important topics, it can be said in order to learn it permanently, you need to forget it three times!

What does it take to be a good math teacher?

Many class teachers feel under-confident in their own math skills, and, in some cases, have had traumatic experiences with math when they were in school. Often, this results in the teacher developing an antipathy towards math. However, if a teacher has had bad experiences with math in his own schooling, it can work to his advantage when teaching math. That teacher may be motivated to "do it differently" and ultimately be determined to find a way to ensure that the class won't have the same negative experiences. Additionally, if such a teacher can find a way to rise above his antipathy toward math, then that teacher may find a newfound joy in math, which can result in bringing math lessons to the children with wonderful enthusiasm.

Still, we should answer the question: "What makes a good math teacher?" We believe that the following list includes the most critical elements:

- The teacher needs to be enthusiastic about learning math. For many teachers, this amounts to finding a new relationship to math. How wonderful it can be to find out that math can be interesting and rewarding!
- The teacher needs to be able to present the material effectively. This is the art of teaching.
- The teacher needs adequate time to prepare for the math lessons. For many teachers, this is the most difficult issue. With everything that is demanded of the class teacher, there often isn't enough time left to prepare adequately for the math lessons.
- The teacher must have a healthy relationship to the students. This helps create a safe and comfortable learning environment for the students.

Of course, it should be noted that the above list could really apply to any subject; math is really no different in this regard.

Communication with parents

The character, commitment, and attitudes of any parent group can vary widely from school to school, and even from class to class. The interests and concerns of a pioneering school are very different from that of a well-established school. For any school, clear communication is critically important. However, given that Waldorf schools tend to attract fairly critical parents, communication needs to be even better than elsewhere. Yet, it often isn't. Many problems at many Waldorf schools have been exacerbated by poor communication.

Parents need to be informed what we are doing and why we are doing it. Beyond simple information exchange, there need to be clear lines of communication to allow parents to express concerns and to allow for discussion and conflict resolution. All of this may seem obvious, but is easier said than done.

In terms of our role as a class teacher, we need to keep parents informed about what is going on in our classroom. This is particularly important when we are doing something out of the ordinary – different than what the parents might expect. For example, in second grade, it would be best to inform the parents *why* we want to keep the children in horizontal form with addition and subtraction and why we don't introduce carrying and borrowing until third grade.

Thoughts on Teaching Lower Grades Math

Teaching the "Big Topics"

Given that our key focus in grades one through four is (1) to develop a sense of number, and (2) to have the students learn their arithmetic facts by heart, much of what is said here regarding the "big topics" (e.g., fractions, percents, algebra, etc.) is more of a concern in fifth grade and up. In short, there are two common mistakes made with teaching the "big topics":

Too much too soon. Often it is said that "fourth grade is fractions"; "fifth grade is decimals", etc. Teachers are then misled into thinking that this one topic should be the central theme and dominate the math lessons for the year. Take the example of fractions in fourth grade. Yes, it is important to introduce fractions in fourth grade. Many teachers do this well. But too often, much of the rest of fourth grade consists of going deeper and deeper into fractions, and then, after a while, much of the class drowns. It may not be recognizable that so many are drowning because on the surface they are "doing" many fraction problems and getting the right answers. For example, they may have been taught a method whereby they can follow the procedure for doing a problem like $7¼ - 2⅔$, but often they get "lost" in process (even if they do all the correct steps and get the right answer) because they lose sight of what the problem actually was. The real goal with fourth grade fractions should only be to have the students develop an enthusiasm for fractions and to have them really understand the fundamental concepts of fractions. The trickier aspects of fractions can be covered in the coming years.

Not enough follow-up and review. Often Waldorf teachers do an excellent job introducing a topic in a very thoughtful and creative way, but then it is dropped – forever. Measurement is a classic example. The class is taught a wonderful main lesson on measurement in third grade and then it isn't touched upon again until middle school. Instead, it should be reviewed and deepened (perhaps only briefly) every year. If we want the students to learn something permanently, then we need to create a "dance" between introducing, deepening, practicing, sleeping, and reviewing.

Timing the introduction to a new topic

All too often, if a teacher were asked, "Why are you teaching this topic to your students now?" the response would be, "Because that's what everyone does!" An example is borrowing. Most teachers introduce borrowing (and have the children practice it a great deal) in second grade. Why? "Because that's when everyone does it." We should instead ask, "When is the best time to introduce borrowing?"

If a topic is introduced too early, or studied too deeply and too soon, then two things are likely to happen: many students in the class will get left behind, and even the ones that can keep up will end up simply doing things mechanically without understanding what they are doing. They are then simply following blind procedures instead of developing strategies, developing mental arithmetic skills, and developing flexibility in thinking. The other extreme – introducing a topic too late – is also problematic. It is best to take the middle road and look for the developmentally appropriate time to bring the topic to the students. Then they will learn the material more deeply, in less time, and with wonderful enthusiasm.

Generally, we should ask the question, "Why do we do what we do, and when should we do it?" As teachers we need to be able to articulate our answer to this important question to ourselves, to our colleagues, and to our parents. Our answers need to be soundly based upon the pedagogical principles of Waldorf education, and upon the developmental stage and needs of the children.

Regarding main lesson

The main lesson is a central aspect of Waldorf education. In general, the following are some of the key ideas to keep in mind when creating a main lesson for the day:

The rhythm of daily activities may be something like this (note that the times may vary):

- *Greeting the children.* This is a time for shaking the children's hands and having a (perhaps quick) check-in with each individual child before the day begins. (Time: 10 minutes)
- *Warm-up.* This can include morning verse, songs, poems/recitation, rhythmical exercises, and other exercises related to the subject of the main lesson. The entire warm-up part of the day's main lesson need only take about 25 minutes in first grade and even less time in older grades.[20]
- *Daily review.* The review component of the daily main lesson should enkindle enthusiasm for what they heard the previous day. We will then build something new on top of this review. (Time: 10 minutes)
- *New material.* Every day the students should experience at least a little something new! (Time: 15 minutes)

---

[20] Else Gottgens, *Joyful Recognition.*

Thoughts on Teaching Lower Grades Math

- *Practice*. During any math main lesson, we should include daily practice of the material from the current block, previous blocks, and previous grades. (Time: 30 minutes or more in fourth and fifth grade, less in earlier grades)
- *Main lesson bookwork*. The children should work with material from the previous day(s) and create beautiful work that they can be proud of. (Time: 20 minutes)
- *Story*. This is simply the story material for the specific grade (i.e., fables/legends in second grade, old testament in third grade, Norse mythology in fourth, and Greek mythology in fifth). (Time: 15-20 minutes)

<u>Flexibility and balance</u>. The amount of time that we spend on each main lesson activity (e.g., *warm-up, review and practice, bookwork*, etc.) may vary from day to day. Maybe the students need to do certain parts of a movement exercise a few more times, or sing a particular song again, or perhaps they need more practical work. When we see that the class becomes sleepy, restless, or not engaged anymore, we have to adjust. If they look pale, then it may be because there has been too much intellectual or memory work going on. If they have very red cheeks, then it may be because there has been too much imagination, drawing etc. Instead, we try to strike a balance – we like to see rosy cheeks!

<u>Breathing and Movement</u>. It is very important to have a healthy in-breathing and out-breathing rhythm every day during main lesson. The teacher should use the main lesson material to keep the children moving throughout the morning. It may not be best to put all of the movement at the beginning of the main lesson. It is often best to "read" the students and look for the moments in the lesson when they need some movement.

<u>Starting a new main lesson block</u>. On the first day of a main lesson, we shouldn't start a block with a review of old material from previous blocks. Instead, we should start with something completely new which catches the enthusiasm and curiosity of the students about the new topic. Review of old material should be appropriately woven into the lessons in the following days.

<u>Main lesson books</u>.
- *The student's creation*. In Waldorf schools, we don't give the students a textbook; they create their own book. The main lesson book is every student's self-made textbook!
- *Progression*. A main lesson book should reflect the progress of the lessons over the course of the four weeks. The new concepts should be clearly written down. A parent should be able to follow the line of thought that the teacher has led the class through.
- *No practice problems* should be written in the main lesson book! The students should have a separate practice book. The work in the practice book should also be quite neat.
- *Pride*. It is very important that the students (in all grades!) take pride in their main lesson books.
- *Beauty*. The books should be done beautifully. It is important to teach the students, starting in first grade, how to create a beautiful book. This includes borders, layout, titles, use of color, etc. While this artistic component is important, remember that the content is even more important.
- *Completion*. There is a tendency in some classes for students not to complete their books and for teachers to even leave a main lesson unfinished. This is very unfortunate! It is very important for students to complete their work. This builds good habits for years into the future. The teacher should frequently check the students' books, so the students get feedback during the block.
- *Corrections*. Starting from first grade, it is important that the teacher reads each student's book and ensures that the student corrects any mistakes.
- *Reference*. Starting in fourth grade, the students should be able to use their main lesson books as a reference.

Stories and pictures

The way in which a topic is introduced is very important; this is the strength of many Waldorf teachers. With a mathematics lesson, however, the teacher needs to keep in mind that the stories, pictures, and images that we create for the child will likely be associated with this topic for a long while. For this reason, a story used to introduce a math topic ought to be shorter and less elaborate than most other stories. Most importantly, the story should help the students understand the essence of the concept being taught. Then, at the right time, the story should fade away, allowing for the mathematical concept to be discussed and practiced in its pure form without the framework of the story. This is because we don't want the children to become too dependent upon the story; they need to understand the essence of the concept. It should also be kept in mind that not all math topics need to be introduced with a story. Telling a story about gnomes collecting a large number of gems and needing to develop a method of counting may be quite helpful for introducing place value to second graders, but it may not be helpful to have an elaborate story to introduce long division – it may actually make long division harder for the children to learn.

Additionally, we should be conscious of our use of a visual picture when introducing a math concept. As teachers, we must be careful to ensure that topics of pure number such as arithmetic, fractions, percents, etc., are developed in the child's mind as free as possible from physical pictures. This doesn't mean that such pictures can never be used. Fractions are more than just pizza, but later we can point out that dividing a pizza is one way to see a fraction. Using manipulatives to help learn addition can be very helpful, but the students also need to see addition done in many ways, never becoming overly reliant on any one physical representation.

If the teacher is cognizant of all of this, it can help the students to better reach the pure concept behind the particular mathematical topic.

Regarding number lines and manipulatives

The number line may be introduced at the end of first grade and then periodically through second grade as one of several different manipulatives. Number lines, like any manipulative, should not be overused, otherwise the children could rely on that one manipulative too much, and then it could inhibit the child from getting to the pure number concept. Instead, by seeing things in many different ways, the child can then come to understand the pure concept more deeply, and, in the process, become more flexible with his thinking.

It is perhaps best for the number line to be phased out at some point in second grade. We recommend that the number line not be used to introduce negative numbers in seventh grade. In fact, after second grade, it could be just fine for the student to not see a number line again until the introduction to Cartesian geometry (i.e., graphing equations) in high school.

In general, manipulatives should be used rarely after second grade for the purpose of learning number concepts and basic arithmetic. Of course, manipulatives do serve quite a useful purpose with more "physical" math topics like measurement and many topics in geometry.

Daily math practice

In grades one through five, math lessons consist of an interweaving of review, rhythmical exercises, daily practice and bookwork. We recommend doing math practice every school day throughout the year. As a general guideline, this math practice should take about 20 to 30 minutes per day during a math block and 10 minutes per day during other blocks. The material for daily math practice comes from the current block (when the class is in a math block), previous blocks, and previous grades.

Be aware of tricks!

Too often, students are taught *blind tricks* as a means for solving a math problem while having no idea why or how the trick works. We believe that such blind tricks should generally be avoided. However, the same trick could be taught in a better way such that the students understand what is behind the trick – or, better yet, the trick may be a shortcut that the students discovered for themselves. This should be our goal; it then has become a *strategic trick* instead of a blind trick. Even if the discovery of the trick is led by a few of the "quicker" students in the class, it is valuable for the whole class to see that it comes from a process.

For example, consider this problem: Convert $4\,^3/_5$ into an improper fraction. If the students are just told that you need to multiply 4 times 5 and then add 3, then it becomes a *blind trick* because they don't have an understanding of what they are doing. However, if they have been led through the process with the teacher, and the class as a whole has come to an understanding of why it works, then this trick has become part of a strategy.

Other tricks include: borrowing, dividing with fractions (i.e., when you flip the second fraction and multiply), and cross-canceling when multiplying fractions.

Again, it's not that these tricks can't be done with the children. The point here is that rather than having the teacher introduce a trick by telling children what the trick is, the children should feel that they played a part in the discovery of the trick. This makes the difference between a "blind trick" and a "strategic trick".

Developing flexibility in thinking

Unfortunately, many students have the impression that for any given math problem there is only one correct answer and one way to derive it. Math is then seen as a rigid and unimaginative subject. We must then look for opportunities to counter this impression. This is one aspect of the wisdom of working from the whole to the part. During a first grade math lesson, if we ask, "What is 12?", think of all the possible correct answers!: 4x3, 6x2, 9+3, 15–3, etc. Then in second grade, it can be fascinating to ask the students how they can calculate 23–15. In fourth grade, the teacher can show different ways to do long division – perhaps there is a parent in the class from another country who can demonstrate how he was taught to do long division. In these ways, the students can then see that math is flexible, creative and imaginative. This also makes math more interesting for the students, helps to develop flexibility in their thinking and, in turn, furthers their sense of number.

Different levels, and avoiding the "Great Divide"

We can feel pressured to have our math class move more quickly and show that "my class is indeed doing advanced math". By doing this, we may impress a few parents and colleagues, and it may make some of the quicker students happy, but we are much more likely then to overwhelm some students and increase the disparity between the stronger and weaker students. This will also likely lead to more students relying upon blind procedures rather than understanding the concepts. (See *Math Trauma* above.)

By fourth grade, the level between the students usually begins to widen. Hopefully, every student is comfortable at his own level. We need to be careful that we don't increase this "divide". All too often, classes enter middle school with a "great divide" between those who are good at math and those who are traumatized by math. Usually, this extreme situation can be avoided. The key to avoiding the great divide is to make sure the "slower" students aren't getting lost and overwhelmed.

But then the question that can be asked is: "What about the quicker students? Won't they be bored?" A few things can be said about this. First of all, in the lower grades, when a student says: "math is easy", it usually isn't really a complaint. That student is usually quite pleased with understanding the material so well. And often, when a student in second or third grade is complaining about being bored, there may be something else going on. It could have something to do with being exposed to media at home – too much fast and short visual impressions through TV or computers can make it difficult for students to think and concentrate at school. Some students are so used to being entertained all day that they cannot entertain themselves, making school seem boring in comparison.

However, the quicker students also need challenges (especially after third grade); it is important to keep these students engaged. The students shouldn't always be doing the exact same thing. At times, we should give different problems to students of different levels so that the "slower" students don't get overwhelmed and the quicker students are adequately challenged. For example, with a practice sheet that has vertical arithmetic problems like 73+45, we could add a few challenge problems, like 5736+2658, at the end. Or, from time to time, the quicker student can help out a fellow classmate. Or maybe a student needing "something extra" can even make up a math sheet for the next day.

This is all part of the art of teaching: How can we reach our goals without losing the students that tend to struggle?

Be aware of using math in a competitive way!

While games and competition can be fun for many of the students, they can leave a few students feeling badly. For this reason, we encourage teachers to be very discerning about what games they bring into the classroom. Simply ask yourself, "Could this game make someone feel badly?" We especially discourage games where students are required to stand up in front of the class (e.g., math-around-the-world, or math-baseball) and compete against one another. For some students, to lose in front of everyone in this way can be quite humiliating. On the other hand, a simple math board game played between friends could be fun and instructive.

In a similar way, we discourage posting in the classroom a list with names of the students who have mastered certain times tables. Imagine how the last one feels!

Additionally, before fifth grade, it is good to find ways to keep it a secret who is taking the longest to complete their math practice sheets. One way to do this is to instruct the students to immediately begin another task (e.g., reading a book) quietly at their desk so that it isn't obvious who the slowest students are. It can also be fine to allow only a certain period of time to work on a practice sheet or a set of problems – when the time is up, then the students stop working. It's fine if some students get further along than others.

Regarding testing

In mainstream education, standardized testing has become more important than ever. Indeed, it drives much of what is done in the classroom. We believe that such testing is detrimental to the children and to the learning process. The major purpose of "testing" should be that the teacher is informed of the students' progress. In this sense, we should be "testing" every day (e.g., through oral exercises and practice sheets – and keep our own records of the students' progress), but the students (even into middle school) should never be conscious of any testing. We should create an attitude in the students, beginning in the early grades, such that they naturally want to do their best – to show their teacher, and themselves, how much they have learned.

What to do when things aren't going well...

- Relax. Parents are often fearful. This gets through to the students and pressures the teacher, who in turn becomes fearful and anxious. Try not to have your teaching driven by anxiety and fear.
- Parent communication. Speak to parents, in parent evenings, and individually. Parents need to understand clearly what you are doing and why, especially if it is different than the norm. Parents need to be well informed. They need to know what their child has achieved and what their child needs to work on.
- Ask yourself: "Why am I doing this?" The answer shouldn't be: "because that's how everyone does it." We should have a real pedagogical answer that we can give to ourselves, our parents, and our colleagues.
- Give it a rest. Re-evaluate what you're doing. Doing more isn't necessarily helpful. Maybe if a particular topic is put to rest for a month or two – or even until next year – then the class will really absorb it better at that later time.
- Make sure that the timing is right. When should we introduce a certain topic? The question shouldn't be "How soon can I do it?", but rather, "Is this the developmentally appropriate time to bring this topic?" Live into where the children are developmentally. If it seems that many of the students aren't ready for something, then it may be wise to listen to that instinct. *When in doubt, wait!*
- Remember your role. Remember that one of our important roles is as "math coach" – to help these children through their emotional math issues.

Working with struggling students

Four steps towards math trauma

- Confusion. *Everyone experiences confusion* when learning math. We can think of confusion as the state you are in as you are working toward clarity. Therefore, confusion is necessary as you are learning something new. Students who are deemed to be "good at math" are usually comfortable with being confused, while for other students, being confused can be bring up many emotions, which may inhibit learning.
- Struggling. *Most students struggle* with math at least occasionally. Normally, when learning a new math topic, the period of confusion should be fairly short. If not, then students may struggle for a period of time until clarity is achieved. In general, one of our goals (especially in middle school and high school) is for all of the students to experience struggle and learn how to work through it.
- Frustration. *Many students get frustrated* with math. Typically, students become frustrated after struggling for an extended period of time. Some students get to the level of frustration almost as soon as they get confused. For many of these students, we need to help them learn to cope with their frustration without taking it personally ourselves.
- Shutting down/trauma. *Some students shut down and become math traumatized.* After a while, if a student is constantly frustrated with math and doesn't ever quite understand the concepts, then he starts to believe that it's impossible and gives up.

One of the jobs of a class teacher is to guide the students through the challenges they encounter in school and in life. In today's world, our children are often shielded from discomfort; they come to expect that things should be easy. They have little patience. It is therefore not surprising that so many children have little tolerance for confusion and struggle. If we compound this with a variety of emotional issues, then we can see how important it is for us, as teachers, to *coach* these students through these challenges.

Perfectionism and fear of failure

Some students have a tendency towards perfectionism. Often it is a girl who wants everything to be in order. Often, it is one of the stronger students in the class. Perfectionists want life to be rhythmical and predictable. And in terms of schoolwork, they want to do well in everything. When faced with a task, they need to be confident that they can do it.

The core of the difficulty is that math often violates these rules. Confusion and learning to overcome your struggles is part of doing math. To some degree, especially in middle school and above, math is about facing the unknown and figuring out how to solve unfamiliar problems. To a perfectionist, all of this is threatening.

Thoughts on Teaching Lower Grades Math

And then the student enters adolescence, becomes more self-aware, and math becomes even more unpleasant and scary. Such a student may eventually just give up on math. Why? Because it is less painful to give up than it is to put forth effort and, in the end, perhaps fail anyway. This is known as "fear of failure".

So what can we do as teachers? Once again, our role as a coach is critical. And this is bigger than just math. We need to look for situations where *they feel they can't succeed*, but *we know they can*. Such a situation could be having a role in a class play, climbing a mountain, riding a bicycle (or a unicycle!), or solving a particularly daunting math problem. They think they can't, and we know they can. At the right time, and in the right way, we need to gently push them into these situations. Our role is to coach them through their challenges, and to help ensure their success. And once they succeed, celebrate! "Look at what you did! And you thought you couldn't do it!" After that, we can build on this success. In this way, the student's confidence is slowly built up, and, over time, the student becomes more comfortable with the challenges that life presents, and hopefully becomes more open to learning math.

Remediation[21]

Meeting the needs of a child with learning challenges can take a good deal of time and energy. In most cases, the problems are in the realm of the lower senses – be it a problem with balance, sense of life and/or gross-motor movement. Often, these children cannot even count one step while saying "one". This makes it more difficult for them to develop a sense of number.

In general, we can always expect to have students who are somewhat behind the rest of the class. In this case, it is especially important for the teacher to know where the child is at, to understand why there is an issue, and to have a plan of how to move forward.

Confidence is an important factor. We need to figure out where the child gets stuck and pick it up from there, so the child starts to build confidence. The student needs to know that his teacher believes in him. The child shouldn't feel that he is doing "dumbed-down math". If the child (or the class as a whole) is behind or has certain holes in his knowledge, then we still have to find ways to bring the current material to him.

Dealing with all of this shouldn't just fall on the shoulders of the class teacher. There are often additional hindrances that obstruct the learning of math. As a faculty, we can work together (e.g., with *child study*) to figure out what is behind this.

Individual *coaching* often makes a huge difference. The class teacher should ask the remedial teacher for help early on; waiting until fifth grade is too late. Any emotional damage takes significant time to heal and can further delay the child's progress with math. Some children with remedial needs (especially if we are able to work with the situation effectively) can be behind the rest of the class for years, but then they can "wake up" to math in a later grade – maybe in fifth grade, or even as late as eighth grade.

Additionally, we need to be careful not to allow fear to set in with ourselves, the student, or the parents – fear exacerbates the situation. We need to work productively with the parents of a child with remedial needs. Clear communication with parents is critical. This includes having a written record (as a school document) of the child's progress and a written record of any modifications in the child's program (i.e., an ILP).

Depending upon a school's resources, it may not be feasible to keep a child with serious learning challenges in the school. Sometimes, in spite of our own emotional attachments to the child, we have to admit that we can't meet a child's needs.

---

[21] For more ideas on working with children with learning challenges, see Ernst Schuberth's book, *Teaching Mathematics for First and Second Grades in Waldorf Schools*, pages 59 and on.

Golden rules

Healthy Math

- <u>Choose developmentally appropriate material</u>. Is the material meeting the children? How does this topic affect the children developmentally?
- <u>When in doubt, wait</u>. Would the children be more able to receive this if you waited until later?
- <u>Less is more</u>! Are you overdoing a new topic? Are you simply "plowing through" the material?
- <u>Minimize blind procedures and tricks</u>. Are the students blindly following procedures and doing tricks without understanding? If so, could this be done differently?

Healthy Students

- <u>Enthusiastic students</u>. Are the students interested and enthused?
- <u>Challenging the students</u>. Are you challenging the students appropriately?
- <u>Avoiding trauma</u>. Are they getting it? Is it too much for some? Are some students' confidence and enthusiasm being damaged? Is the learning environment healthy, so that students can learn?

Healthy Teacher

- <u>Enthusiastic teacher</u>. Are you interested and enthused?
- <u>Health and balance</u>. Are you healthy and balanced with a strong inner life?
- <u>Relationship to the material</u>. Are you the author of what you bring to the class? Are you clear about why you are teaching this topic now to these students? Do you see the "big picture"?
- <u>Relationship with the children</u>. The material is not the most important thing. What matters is how you bring it, who you are in front of the children, and your relationship with the children.

−First Grade Math−

Overview of Child Development in First Grade

With the change of teeth, the capacity of thinking reveals itself, and the desire to learn and to follow a beloved authority becomes apparent. Instead of imitating the surrounding world at will, the children focus more on following their teacher. Thus, the first school year is still marked by a "dreaming living" in the world. This is a ripple effect from the early childhood years. There is an eagerness for learning and the children want to engage through their feelings. They connect with the subject matter through rhymes, music, movement, etc. Through images, the spoken word enlivens the inner thinking of the children. As their teacher, we want them to work willingly, and we use images to motivate them. Instead of saying: "Write your numbers straight", we say: "Let all your numbers stand as straight as a spear." Of course, all the work should be presented with joy and enthusiasm.

For teaching math in first grade, this means we use stories (e.g., a baker who makes muffins and puts them into rows of two, or on plates in groups of four, or he sells them in groups of three). The students illustrate these stories in their main lesson books. The teacher can vary things every day while working with the same concept and story.

Curriculum Summary for First Grade Math

The world of numbers
- *Roman numerals.* We begin with the Roman numerals because they are related to the human body. The (standard) Arabic numbers can be introduced afterwards.
- *Quality of numbers.* What is the quality of numbers that we see in the world?
- *Counting.* Practice counting forward and backward to 100. The children need to become "at ease"[22] with this.
- *Number dictations.* Number dictations should start in the second math block.

Developing a sense of number
- The sense for numbers is awakening. The goal in first grade is for the children to come to conscious counting through movement. Else Gottgens calls this "counting along the line".[23]
- *Whole to the part.* As mentioned in the introduction, working from the whole to the part is an important aspect of our work. This is especially true in first grade. For example, instead of always asking questions like, "What is 9+3?", we can instead ask, "What is 12?" Think of the possibilities!
- The children should gradually come to see a number as an entity in itself. This is important! Can they immediately recognize a group of five on a dice, a flash of three fingers, or a group of six nuts? The children can make their own flashcards from these examples.
- *Rhythmical counting.* Rhythmical counting serves as preparation for learning the times tables in second grade. In first grade, the children learn to do rhythmical counting by 2's, 3's, 4's, 5's, 10's, and 11's. This work should come out of the imagination. In first grade, we should always count by ones, but emphasize the given number. For example, with rhythmical counting by 3's, we count forwards and backwards while emphasizing every third number, perhaps by clapping and saying it louder: 1, 2, **3**, 4, 5, **6**, 7, 8, **9**, 10, 11, **12**, etc. We don't need to mention that this is the 3's times table; we simply call it rhythmical counting by 3's. No rhythmical counting is done in first grade between the math main lessons – it goes to sleep during those time periods.
- *Movement.* Math is related to the physical body. In order to get an awareness of mathematical processes, the children need to move their body. For many first graders, it is a challenge to synchronize their movement with their voice. Their voice is usually faster than the movement of either their hands or their feet.
- *Estimating.* We can ask: "How many steps am I from the board?" or "How many giant steps am I from the door?" In this way, the child tries to find his position in the world, which helps to develop a spatial orientation.

---

[22] Throughout this book, we use the following terms: "Fluent" means they need to have it on the tip of their tongues without any hesitation. "At/with ease" means they need to feel comfortable but there might still be some hesitation. Therefore, we have three stages in learning a skill: Introduction, "at ease", and "fluent".

[23] Else Gottgens, *Waldorf Education in Practice*, page 35.

First Grade Math

Beginning calculations
- *Regrouping numbers.* For example, how can we regroup the number ten? There are many answers: 2 groups of five, five groups of two, 6 and 4, 7 and 3, etc.
- *Introducing the four processes.* The students should be fluent with sums (e.g., 8+5) up to 24, and with ease up to 100.
- *Learning the "easy" addition facts.* All addition facts up to 10, as well as all of the doubles (i.e., 6+6, 7+7, 8+8, 9+9) should be learned by heart by the end of first grade.

Recommended Reading for First Grade Math
- Henning Anderson, *Active Arithmetic.* AWSNA Publications.
- Herman von Baravalle, *The Teaching Of Arithmetic And The Waldorf School Plan.* Waldorf School Monographs, 1967, third edition.
- Irene Groh, Mona Ruef, and the Medical Section at the Goetheanum, *Education and Teaching as Preventive Medicine.* Persephone, Forest Row 2006, pages 117-131.
- Ernst Schuberth, *Teaching Mathematics for First and Second Grades in Waldorf Schools.* Rudolf Steiner College Press.
- Rudolf Steiner, *The Spiritual Ground of Education,* chapter 5. Anthroposophic Press.
- Rudolf Steiner, *The Kingdom of Childhood,* chapter 5. Anthroposophic Press.

Lessons and Topics for First Grade Math

"It is especially important not to go on working in a monotonous way, doing nothing but adding for six months, etc., but where possible one should take all four arithmetic rules fairly quickly one after another and then practice them…We should take all four rules at once and be careful that through practice these four rules are mastered almost at the same time."
--Rudolf Steiner (from Stockmeyer's book)

Background reading. Be sure to reread the section, *Thoughts on Teaching Math in the Lower Grades,* found at the start of this book.

Mental arithmetic. Mental arithmetic is integrated into the math lessons through the use of imaginative number stories.

Scheduling
The curriculum calls for 12 weeks of math in first grade, usually one main lesson block at the end of October, one in January, and one in March. A one-week review of math can be done at the year's end.

Math Main Lesson Block #1
Content overview
- *Quality of the numbers 1-12,* with Roman and Arabic numerals. Find an image for every number, perhaps using an ongoing story where the central question is: Where is there only one of something in the world? Where is there two? Where is there three, etc?
- *Counting.* Practice counting up to 24 (forward and backward) with ease, and up to 100 with joy!
- *Rhythmical counting.* During this first block, we can do rhythmical counting by 2's and 4's. We should practice going both forwards and backwards.
- *Regrouping.* The idea of regrouping is briefly introduced here. It quite naturally comes out of our work with going from the whole to the part. (E.g., "How can we regroup the number ten?" There are many answers: 2 groups of five, five groups of two, 6 and 4, 7 and 3, etc.)
- *Writing.* Practice writing the numbers 1-12. Always start at the top (of the digit's written form) and draw towards the bottom.
- *The four processes.* The four processes (+, –, x, ÷) are briefly introduced, but only orally. (In the second math block the students write them down for the first time.)

First Grade Math

Movement
- Speaking and moving should go together. This is very important for the development capacities.[24]
- Count from 1-24. Practice counting by using one step per number, using images. For e̵x̵ children imagine going over stepping-stones across a river, or dwarfs stepping into a dark c̵ they collect gems, jewels, etc. Have them then walk and count backwards as they go back home again.
- Rhythmical counting. (Hopping, clapping, stamping, etc.) Here are some examples:
  - For counting by two's, the dwarfs move the axes rhythmically: 1, **2**, 3, **4**, 5, **6**, 7, **8**, 9, **10**, etc.
  - *Even and odd numbers.* The farmer who lost one wooden shoe in the heavy clay: Because the farmer (and the children) only have one shoe on, we can only hear one of the steps clearly. It goes like this: 1, **2**, 3, **4**, 5, etc., where we whisper the 1,3,5 and speak loudly the other ones. Of course, the children can use boots instead of wooden shoes! On the next day, the farmer might lose the other shoe/boot, so we would count the odd numbers instead.
  - *Very important!* After we have finished a movement, the children should stand still and say the sequence of numbers once again, forward and backwards without movement. In this way, we bring the will activity to consciousness.

Working with manipulatives
- Counting should be connected to an object, starting with their own fingers and toes. Different objects may be: chestnuts, gems, etc. Try to avoid counting with food (beans, lentils, etc.). Unless you are eating it, food is not something to play with in a world where there is hunger.
- *Regrouping numbers.* The children put both of their hands on their desk, and we ask the students to show four fingers in the air with one hand. We can then ask: how many different ways are there to show four fingers if you can use both hands? (One way would be one finger on one hand and three fingers on the other hand.)
- The teacher can also hold up four fingers, and the child needs to immediately recognize that there are four fingers. This demands a lot of practice as the children learn to move away from counting. This can also be done by using different objects on a table under a cloth, etc. For examples, imagine using a certain amount of chestnuts. We show them very briefly and then cover them up. We then ask the children how many chestnuts they saw. The idea is that we want them to see the amount immediately instead of counting every single nut. This can also be done using flashcards.
- *The five-structure.* This is also the first visual encounter with the five-structure. The five-structure is the five fingers on our hands; two hands make ten. It is easy for most children to work with units of five. This becomes quite useful later when we start to develop strategies. It is perhaps the first strategy they will use.
- We should also ask the students to regroup a number of gems. For example, using 12 gems, there are many possibilities:

  *** *** *** ***   or   ** ** ** ** ** **   or   **** **** ****   or   ***** ** * ****

- Making geometrical forms with the manipulatives. In Henning Anderson's book[25], he has the children draw a circle on a piece of paper and then asks them to put three (or perhaps another number) chestnuts somewhere on the circle. There are different possibilities, but most students try to find a harmony and will make a perfect equilateral triangle. Rudolf Steiner also writes about the importance of these activities[26].

Review and practice
- *The importance of review.* We must emphasize here, once again, the importance of how the teacher must be conscious of using the child's sleep life as part of the learning process. The teacher must review (i.e., bring back into the child's imagination) the new material from the previous day, perhaps by

---

[24] Else Gottgens, *Waldorf Education in Practice*, page 37.
[25] Henning Anderson, *Active Arithmetic*. AWSNA Publications.
[26] Rudolf Steiner, *The Child's Changing Consciousness*. Lecture given on April 17, 1923. GA 306.

using different materials. We might regroup 12 children, and then the next day, during the review, we might regroup 12 chairs.
- *Writing numbers.* We should practice writing numbers in a sand tray, on paper, using small blackboards, or go outside and practice writing numbers with sticks. Remember to always have the children write the numbers from top to bottom!
- We should practice movement exercises with counting every day, but each day we use different variations. For example, we can imagine 12 dwarfs going into a cave, while the rest of the students are fireflies watching them. In this way, some students are observing what the others are doing. This brings a different consciousness to the process. Once again, we expect to see that movement while simultaneously speaking can be quite difficult.
- *Regrouping.* After the number 12 has been reviewed, we practice the same regrouping with a different number.

Bookwork
- In this block, the children can make drawings in their books from the qualities of the first 12 numbers. They can write the twelve Roman numerals here, and perhaps the Arabic numerals simultaneously as well.
- The children's main lesson book should include a few examples of number regrouping.
- Be sure to visit our website (**www.JamieYorkPress.com**) to see full-color pages from students' main lesson books.

Math Main Lesson Block #2

Content overview
- *The four processes.* In the first math main lesson, the four processes were briefly introduced orally, but they weren't written down. Now, for the first time, the four processes are written down.
- *Counting.* The children should now be able to count with ease up to 100.
- *Rhythmical counting.* During this second block, we should review rhythmical counting by 2's and 4's, and then add the 5's, 10's and 3's. Remember to practice going both forwards and backwards. How far we get with this work depends upon the abilities of the class.
- *Regrouping.* We should continue our work started in the first main lesson with regrouping numbers.
- *Writing.* We continue what we started during the first math block. Remember to always write the numbers from the top (of the digit's written form) progressing to the bottom. We can now start doing some number dictations up to 24.

New material
- *Introduction of the four processes.*
  - Each process (plus, minus, times, and divide) is introduced through four characters, each having one of the four temperaments.[27] Addition (plus) is phlegmatic, keeping as much as possible; subtraction (minus) is melancholic, carelessly losing things; multiplication (times) is sanguine, working as quickly as possible; and division (divide) is choleric, sharing everything fairly.
  - Of course, the children have already worked with these four processes through regrouping activities and through our math stories during our first math block. But now we introduce the signs of the four processes (+, –, x, ÷) visually.
  - Addition and multiplication are introduced from the whole to the parts.
    - Example: 8 = 5 + 3.
    - Example: 14 = 2 x 7
  - Subtraction starts from the difference.
    - Example: A girl picks flowers in the field. She brings 12 flowers home, but she counts only 9 flowers. How many flowers did she lose?

---

[27] Ernst Schuberth, *Teaching Mathematics for First and Second Grades in Waldorf Schools.* page 34-48. Also, Dorothy Harrer, *Math Lessons For Elementary Grades.* AWSNA Publications.

First Grade Math

- Likewise, division starts from the quotient.
  - Example: 12 rabbits were playing in the field and suddenly the fox appeared. The rabbits ran to their homes, but there were only 3 homes, and every home could only have the same number of rabbits. This is also a social activity.
    At the end of the game we bring this problem to consciousness. So we can write:
    12=4+4+4 or 12=3x4 or 12÷3=4 or 12–4–4–4=0 (Then there are no rabbits left.)
- During this block, we play with these concepts using the four processes.

Movement
- In the first math main lesson block, we did a counting movement using the image of a farmer with one wooden shoe. Now we can create new stories that call for different activities and counting movements.
- We start on a different number (e.g., 12 or 15), and count up from there until 36 or 42. We can also do this backwards. This helps the students to become confident with moving up and down past the tens (i.e., past 20, 30, 40, etc.).
  - Example: 27, 28, 29, 30, 31, 32, 33, 34, 35, 36, 36, 35, 34, 33, 32, 31, 30, 29, 28, 27.
- *Rhythmical counting*. Practice rhythmical counting with the 2's, 3's, 4's, 5's, 10's, and 11's. Slowly, with the 2's, 3's, and 4's, the students can say only the numbers in the tables (as opposed to earlier in the year when they were saying every number and emphasizing the numbers in the table). With the 5's, 10's, and 11's, the students can immediately jump into counting by 5's, 10's, and 11's.

Working with manipulatives
- Work with regrouping the numbers 1-24, using manipulatives and/or fingers.
- Students can work in pairs. For example, with the number 8, the teacher writes all the different possibilities on the board, and the students find as many regroupings as possible, such as:
  8=2+6   8 = 1+7   8 = 7+1   8 = 4+4
  There are, of course, many more possibilities, but some of them cannot be made with our fingers.
- The next day, review the regrouping that was done yesterday, and then use the T-form to organize it:

  8
  0 | 8
  1 | 7
  2 | 6
  3 | 5   etc.

- Now we can practice with these regroupings in the following way: Using your right hand, cover the section on the right side of the vertical line (we have to show this to the students) and now we will say: "8 is 1 plus what?" (they need to figure out the 7 and they can check it under their hand). Then they move down and say: "8 is 2 plus what?"

Review and practice
- As always, the new material should be reviewed every day.
- Continue practicing writing numbers, and regularly doing number dictations up to 24.
- We should use the T-form (see above) to work with regrouping many different numbers.

Bookwork
- The main lesson book needs to be artistic – much more than just dry numbers.
- Have the children show the use of the T-form to regroup the numbers 1-24 (see above).
- They can begin to include some problems in their books that use the signs (+, –, x, ÷) of the four processes, such as 8=4+4, 8=10–2, 8=2x4, 8÷2=4 etc.
- Have the children draw pictures from the stories in their math lessons, which should include the characters of these stories (e.g., from the fox and rabbit story, Mini Minus, David Divide, etc.). They should also carefully draw the signs for the four processes (+, –, x, ÷).
- Be sure to visit our website (**www.JamieYorkPress.com**) to see full-color pages from students' main lesson books.

First Grade Math

Math Main Lesson Block #3

Content overview

- *Practicing counting.* All students should be very fluent counting (forward and backwards) up to 24, and at ease with counting (forward and backwards) up to 100.
- *The four processes.* All students are becoming fluent with working with the four processes up to 10, and becoming more at ease with the four processes up to 24.
- *Strategies.* Introduce some strategies. This is a preview of a theme carried into second grade. In first grade, these strategies come out of our work with regrouping.
- *Rhythmical counting.* This important work continues what was begun in the first two math blocks. By the end of first grade, it is good for the children to have worked regularly with rhythmical counting with the 2's, 3's, 4's, 5's, 10's, and 11's.

New material

- *Progressing from counting to math.* The children now begin to move beyond counting and learn to think more "mathematically", as they develop more of a sense of number. In this way, they begin to learn strategies for doing calculations, especially involving addition and subtraction. In order to do this, the teacher should be aware of the step-by-step progression for teaching addition, subtraction, etc. (See *A step-by-step progression for addition and subtraction* under *More Ideas for Teaching* below.)
- *Learning the "easy" addition facts.* This requires the use of memory forces. All addition facts up to 10, as well as all of the doubles (i.e., 6+6, 7+7, 8+8, 9+9) should be known by heart by the end of first grade.
- *Strategies for larger facts.* The students should begin to use strategies. For example, with 5+6 we could do 5+5+1 or 6+6–1. Using 12–4 as another example, they could think of it as 12–2–2, or even arrive at the answer by counting by 4's. Since both 4 and 12 are in the 4's table, the answer, 8, is also in the 4's table. It is wonderful for the students to share with the class, the strategies that they have discovered!

Movement

- Previously the whole class did rhythmical counting exercises together. Now we need to do this in small groups and individually too.
- *The four steps for movement exercises.* The following four steps are quite important. Here is an example using 12 + __ = 19.

    Step #1: Have the students stand on 12. How many steps are there to get to 19? In this case they are doing three things: stepping, speaking the numbers (starting with 13), and counting the steps on their fingers. In the end (after reaching 19), we can ask different questions, like: "What is the difference between 12 and 19?", or "12 plus what is 19?", or "What is 19 minus 12?"

    Step#2: The children stand still and speak out loud the same math problem (12 + __ = 19) without moving. They speak the numbers 13, 14, 15, 16, 17, 18, 19 while counting on their fingers each step.

    Step#3: The children sit down and write down what just was spoken. Now they write down the problem: 12 + 7 = 19

    Step#4: The children read back what is written down.

    (The children could also use their small blackboards to practice this.)

- *Rhythmical counting.* Continue practicing rhythmical counting with the 2's, 3's, 4's, 5's, 10's, and 11's. (See *rhythmical counting* above in block #2.) We can now work with the tables more in depth. For example, with the two's, we move the row of two's (2, 4, 6, 8, etc.). The whole class moves it (e.g., walking) forward and backwards. Then the whole class stands still while speaking the row of 2. Then they sit down and from memory write down the row of two's on their little blackboards. Then they read back aloud the row 2, 4, 6, 8, etc.

First Grade Math

Working with manipulatives
- *Fading out manipulatives.* At this point in the first grade year, it is important to get away from working with manipulatives. The students can now imagine the problem and then find ways to solve it.

- *Introducing larger numbers.* With the smaller numbers (up to 24), we try to not use manipulatives at this point, but some children may still need some visual help. We could provide them with a string of 20 wooden beads, colored in the five-structure, as shown with the photo here.

- *Number line.* This can be the right time to bring the number line (up to 100) into the classroom. This should be practiced both ways: saying a number that is pointed at, and finding a number that is spoken.
- *Games.* Try to find engaging games using the number line (see Henning Anderson's book), as well as dice and board games (see the appendix for a list of games for lower school math). These can be wonderful things for the children to do when there is extra time.

Review and practice
- *Number dictations.* We can now do number dictations up to 100.
- *The four processes.* Continue writing and practicing problems that use the four processes.
- *Patterns with numbers.*
    - The children should visualize problems they did with manipulatives in previous blocks.
    - We should continue practicing the regrouping of numbers.
    - Look for ways to show the pattern of numbers. Baravalle's book has many wonderful ideas for this. Here are a couple of examples (using triangular and square numbers – but we don't need to mention these terms to the children):

$$
\begin{aligned}
1 &= 1 \rightarrow \qquad\qquad 1 \\
1+2 &= 3 \rightarrow 3-1 = 2 \\
1+2+3 &= 6 \rightarrow 6-3 = 3 \\
1+2+3+4 &= 10 \rightarrow 10-6 = 4 \\
&\ldots\text{etc.}
\end{aligned}
$$

or

$$
\begin{aligned}
1 &= 1 \rightarrow 1\times1=1 \rightarrow \qquad 1 \\
1+3 &= 4 \rightarrow 2\times2=4 \rightarrow 4-1 = 3 \\
1+3+5 &= 9 \rightarrow 3\times3=9 \rightarrow 9-4 = 5 \\
1+3+5+7 &= 16 \rightarrow 4\times4=16 \rightarrow 16-9 = 7 \\
&\ldots\text{etc.}
\end{aligned}
$$

Bookwork
- Baravalle's book can be a nice guide for the main lesson bookwork.
- Work done with the number line can be put into the students' book in a visual way (e.g., showing rabbits hopping on the line from one number to the next, skipping numbers at times, etc.).
- The children can write all of the numbers from 1-100 in a list into their main lesson books.
- The layout and use of color in the main lesson book is all very important.
- Be sure to visit our website (**www.JamieYorkPress.com**) to see full-color pages from students' main lesson books.

First Grade Math

A step-by-step progression for addition in first grade

Notes:
- Keep in mind that these steps for addition are happening concurrently with a similar step-by-step progression for subtraction (see next page).
- This is intended to give the teacher some possible ideas of what could be done to work in a structured way.
- There are more steps possible than are listed below.

Step #1: Regrouping 10.
  Ask: "What is 10?"
  $10 = 1 + 9$
  $10 = 2 + 8$
  $10 = 3 + 7$
  …etc.

Step #2: Adding to 10.
  $1 + 9 = \_\_$
  $2 + 8 = \_\_$
  $3 + 7 = \_\_$
  …etc.

Step #3: Finding the missing number using 10.
  $10 = 1 + \_\_$
  $10 = 2 + \_\_$
  $10 = \_\_ + 7$
  $10 = \_\_ + 9$
  …etc.

Step #4: Regrouping 20.
  Ask: "What is 20?"
  $20 = 11 + 9$
  $20 = 12 + 8$
  $20 = 13 + 7$
  …etc.

Step #5: Adding to 20, such as:
  $11 + 9 = \_\_$
  $12 + 8 = \_\_$
  $13 + 7 = \_\_$
  …etc.

Step #6: Finding the missing number using 20.
  $20 = 11 + \_\_$
  $20 = \_\_ + 8$
  …etc.

Step #7: Working with doubles.
  $2 = \_\_ + \_\_ \rightarrow 1 + 1 = \_\_$
  $4 = \_\_ + \_\_ \rightarrow 2 + 2 = \_\_$
  …etc. up to $20 = 10 + 10$

Step #8: Add two one-digit numbers for a sum between 11 and 18, such as:
  $11 = 5 + \_\_ \rightarrow 5 + 6 = \_\_$
  $15 = 7 + \_\_ \rightarrow 8 + 5 = \_\_$
  …etc.

Step #9: Add a two-digit number to a one-digit number, up to a sum of 20, such as:
  $10 + 2 = \_\_ \rightarrow 12 = 10 + \_\_$
  $12 + 4 = \_\_ \rightarrow 16 = 12 + \_\_$
  $8 + 12 = \_\_ \rightarrow 20 = 8 + \_\_$
  …etc.

Step #10: Add a two-digit and a one-digit number, for a sum between 21 and 24, such as:
  $15 + 6 = \_\_ \rightarrow 21 = 15 + \_\_$
  $18 + 5 = \_\_ \rightarrow 23 = 18 + \_\_$
  $17 + 7 = \_\_ \rightarrow 24 = 17 + \_\_$
  …etc.

First Grade Math

A step-by-step progression for subtraction in first grade

Notes:
- Keep in mind that these steps for subtraction are happening concurrently with a similar step-by-step progression for addition (see previous page).
- Here again, there are many more steps and variations possible. We would like to encourage teachers to find more steps!!!

Step #1: The first steps.
$1 = 1 - \_\_ \rightarrow 1 - 0 = \_\_$
$1 = 2 - \_\_ \rightarrow 2 - \_\_ = 1$
$1 = 3 - \_\_$ etc.
$2 = 2 - \_\_ \rightarrow 2 - 0 = \_\_$
$2 = 3 - \_\_ \rightarrow 3 - \_\_ = 2$
$2 = 4 - \_\_$ etc.
…etc.

Step #2: Subtracting with 10 and under.
$10 = 10 - \_\_ \rightarrow 10 - 0 = 1\_\_$
$9 = 10 - \_\_ \rightarrow 10 - \_\_ = 9$
$8 = 10 - \_\_$ etc.
$9 = 9 - \_\_ \rightarrow 9 - \_\_ = 9$
$8 = 9 - \_\_ \rightarrow 9 - 1 = \_\_$
$7 = 9 - \_\_$ etc.
$8 = 8 - \rightarrow \_\_ - 0 = 8$
$7 = \_\_ - 1 \rightarrow 8 - 1 = \_\_$
$6 = 8 - \_\_$ etc.
…etc.

Step #3: Subtracting numbers 20 and under with a result of 10, or greater.
$20 = 20 - \_\_ \rightarrow 20 - 0 = \_\_$
$19 = 20 - \_\_ \rightarrow 20 - \_\_ = 19$
$18 = 20 - \_\_$ etc.
$19 = 19 - \_\_ \rightarrow \_\_ - 0 = 19$
$18 = 19 - \_\_ \rightarrow 19 - \_\_ = 18$
$17 = 19 - \_\_$ etc.
$18 = 18 - \_\_ \rightarrow 18 - 0 = \_\_$
$17 = 18 - \_\_ \rightarrow 18 - \_\_ = 17$
$16 = 18 - \_\_$ etc.
…etc.

Step #4: Subtracting a one-digit number from between 11 and 19 with a result less than 10.
$9 = 11 - \_\_ \rightarrow 11 - 2 = \_\_$
$8 = 11 - \_\_ \rightarrow 11 - 3 = \_\_$
$7 = 11 - \_\_$ etc.
$9 = 12 - \_\_ \rightarrow 12 - 3 = \_\_$
$8 = 12 - \_\_ \rightarrow 12 - \_\_ = 8$
$7 = 12 - \_\_$ etc.
$9 = 13 - \_\_ \rightarrow 13 - 4 = \_\_$
$8 = 13 - \_\_ \rightarrow 13 - \_\_ = 8$
$7 = 13 - \_\_$ etc.
…etc.

Step #5: Subtracting a one-digit number from between 21 and 24 with a result less than 20.
$19 = 21 - \_\_ \rightarrow 21 - \_\_ = 19$
$18 = 21 - \_\_ \rightarrow 21 - 3 = \_\_$
$17 = 21 - \_\_$ etc.
$19 = 22 - \_\_ \rightarrow 22 - 3 = \_\_$
$18 = 22 - \_\_ \rightarrow 22 - \_\_ = 18$
$17 = 22 - \_\_$ etc.
$19 = 23 - \_\_ \rightarrow 23 - 4 = \_\_$
$18 = 23 - \rightarrow 23 - 5 = \_\_$
$17 = 23 - \_\_$ etc.
…etc.

Step #6: Finding the difference between two numbers (working with the number 20).
$20 - 11$ (What is the difference b/t 20 & 11?)
$20 - 12$ (What is the difference b/t 20 & 12?)
$20 - 13$ (What is the difference b/t 20 & 13?)
…etc.

Step #7: Finding the difference between two numbers (working between 21 and 24).
$21 - 11$ (What is the difference b/t 21 & 11?)
$21 - 12$ (What is the difference b/t 21 & 12?)
$21 - 13$, etc.
$22 - 11$ (What is the difference b/t 22 & 11?)
$22 - 12$ (What is the difference b/t 22 & 12?)
$22 - 13$, etc.
$23 - 11$ (What is the difference b/t 23 & 11?)
$23 - 12$ (What is the difference b/t 23 & 12?)
$23 - 13$, etc.
…etc.

–Second Grade Math–

Overview of Child Development in Second Grade

The second grader is in the middle of an important developmental phase between the ages of six and nine. It is a golden time where the student is still king in his own kingdom. The second grader is now livelier and more aware of what is happening around him. He may even become mischievous. Physically, the roundness of the early childhood years has disappeared. The mouth is closed and the student becomes less dreamy. The child's personality and character become more evident. We can help the children to overcome the one-sidedness of their character by telling fables and saint stories. The joy of learning is based on strong habits, rhythms, and songs. The creative forces of the child increase along with an ability to create more vivid inner pictures. The second grader's confidence grows and builds upon the foundation laid in grade one. However, the student still needs strong leadership from the teacher through a consistent and rhythmical approach to the lessons. An artistic approach is used to awaken the intellect.

With the math lessons, this is the year to introduce the times tables – all of them brought in an artistic way. The child is eager to show his individual abilities, such as the joy of finding missing numbers, or the discovery of geometrical patterns in the times tables. At this age, the child's memory forces are very strong, so it is an ideal time to begin to learn the arithmetic facts.

Curriculum Summary for Second Grade Math

The world of numbers
- The children should become fluent with counting up to 100. They should be able to start anywhere and continue counting without any hesitation, and do this either counting forward or backward.
- The students should gradually become at ease with the number world up to 1000 (and possibly higher).
- *Estimating*. We build up from the estimating done in first grade and progress to more challenging estimations.

Place value. Place value is introduced and practiced. Be sure that all the children really get this; this is an important step needed in order to deeply understand the world of numbers.

Addition and subtraction facts. By the end of the year, the class should have learned their addition facts (up to 24) and corresponding subtraction facts *by heart*.

The times/division tables
- Beginning in second grade, multiplication and division go together. The times tables and division tables are really the same thing.
- By the end of the year, the class should be comfortable with all of the times and division tables (from 1-12), in a row. This requires daily, systematic work! Be sure to read *A Step-by-Step Progression for the Arithmetic Facts* (in the appendix).

The four processes
- *Addition*. By the end of the year, the class should be *at ease* with adding any two-digit number with a one-digit number (e.g., 57+6).
- *Subtraction*. By the end of the year, the class should be *at ease* with subtracting any one-digit number from a two-digit number (e.g., 52–6), and also with subtracting two 2-digit numbers such that the answer is a one-digit number (e.g., 72–69).
- The students must gain a deeper understanding of the concept of multiplication and division, such as:
  $3 \times 2 = \underline{}$ asks: "Three groups of two makes what?"
  $12 \div 3 = \underline{}$ asks: "How many groups of three fit in twelve?"
- By the end of the year, the children should be able to do all four processes (even alternating on the same page) and know the difference between the processes without help (but keep the problems simple!).
- The introduction to both vertical addition (i.e., carrying) and vertical subtraction (i.e., borrowing) should wait until third grade. Therefore, all written work with the four processes should still be done in horizontal form (e.g., 9=5+4, 5+4=9).

Time orientation. The children should become at ease with the days of the week, the months of the year, and terms like "tomorrow", "yesterday", "noon", "afternoon", "evening", "six o'clock", etc.

Second Grade Math

<u>The wonder of number</u>. Bring wonder and awe to the world of numbers. One way in which this can be done is with the *geometrical patterns* that arise from the relation between times/division tables and the 10-point circle or the 12-point circle. (See more details under Block #1 below.)

Recommended Reading for Second Grade Math

- Henning Anderson, *Active Arithmetic*. AWSNA Publications.
- Herman von Baravalle, *The Teaching Of Arithmetic And The Waldorf School Plan*. Waldorf School Monographs, 1967, third edition.
- Else Gottgens, *Joyful Recognition*.
- Else Gottgens, *Waldorf Education in Practice*.
- Dorothy Harrer, *Math Lessons For Elementary Grades*. AWSNA Publications.
- Christoph Jaffke, *Rhythms, Rhymes, Games and Songs for the Lower School*. Published by the Pedagogische Forschung Stelle, Der Bund der Freien Waldorf Schule in Stuttgart.
- Lipping Ma, *Knowing and Teaching Elementary Mathematics*. Lawrence Erlbaum Assoc. Publishers 1919, London.
- Ernst Schuberth, *Teaching Mathematics for First and Second Grades in Waldorf Schools*. Rudolf Steiner College Press.
- John A. van de Walle, *Elementary and Middle School Mathematics*. Virginia Commonwealth University, Longman, NY.

Lessons and Topics for Second Grade Math

<u>Scheduling</u>

The curriculum calls again for twelve weeks of math. The first math main lesson should fall around October, the second block around January, and the last block falls in the spring. Each block should be four weeks long, and there should be one week of math review at the end of the school year.

Don't forget!!

- *Every day*, we should <u>review</u> the previous day's lesson.
- *Every day*, we should bring <u>something new</u> to the children.
- *Every day*, the students should <u>practice</u> the new material and selected review topics.

Practice and review (of old material)

- Most of the topics listed below were introduced some time ago. In order for the children to learn a topic well, it needs to be systematically reviewed. Obviously, all previous topics cannot be reviewed every day. The teacher needs to decide which topics are the most important to review each day. Some of these topics may need to be reviewed and practiced nearly every day, even when the class is not in a math block – although, it should take no more than a total of 10 minutes.
(Also see *Review and Practice* under *Principles of Waldorf Education* in the *Introduction* above.)

<u>The world of numbers</u>
- *Counting* up to 100 fluently, and up to 1000 at ease – forward and backward. Children should be very comfortable in doing this on their own without help.
- *Number dictations*. Number dictations should be used to help the students become familiar with the larger numbers that come about through the introduction of place value. Dictations should continue after the place value block ends. Students need to feel confident in writing any number between 1-1000.
- *Language*. Be careful when speaking these new, larger numbers (and expect the same of the students), so that an extra "and" isn't added in. For example, 270 should be spoken as "two-hundred-seventy", not "two-hundred-*and*-seventy".

Second Grade Math

...ubtraction facts. By the end of the year, the class should have learned their addition facts (up to ...rresponding subtraction facts *by heart*.

...ctice using strategies for addition and subtraction.
...or example, 24 +13 can be looked at as 24+10 +3 or 20+10+4+3 or 24+6 +7, etc.

Times and division tables
- Remember that times/division tables are the highest priority for math in second grade.
- By the end of the year, the class should be comfortable with all of the times and division tables from 1-12, in a row. This requires daily, systematic work!
- The times tables and the division tables are worked on at the same time. The students can then experience how multiplication and division are related.
- Be sure to read *A Step-by-Step Progression for the Arithmetic Facts* (in the appendix).

Practice with the four processes. The students should continue practicing the four processes daily and develop strategies to solve these problems. The students need to practice a sufficient amount of problems, so that they start to feel confident. Also, try to make the problems interesting. For example, you could work it out so that there is a sequence in the answers, such as

$$18+17 = 35$$
$$21+14 = 35$$
$$29+6 = 35$$

and then, there is suddenly a "little dragon" that has a different answer!
$$16+18 = 34$$

Time. Once the days, months, seasons, and clock time have been covered in main lesson, they should all be reviewed at least briefly, so that the students remain fluent with these concepts.

Mental arithmetic
- Practice mental arithmetic daily (for 10 minutes or less).
- Mental arithmetic also helps the children to become flexible in using the four processes.
- Work up to calculations like $28 + 5$; $14 \div 2$; 8×5; $86 - 3$; $76 - 74$; $42-6$, $72-69$.
- *Halfway problems.* These problems should start off easy in second grade and get increasingly more difficult in the coming years. Some examples are:
  - What number is halfway between 25 and 29?
  - What number is halfway between 5 and 13?
  - What number is halfway between 5 and 23?
  - What number is halfway between 25 and 31?

Word Problems. In second grade, word problems may still be done through imaginative stories, and they can also be done more simply during the mental arithmetic section of the lesson. Here are some examples:
- An empty bus stops and picks up 8 people. At the next stop, 3 people get off and then 4 get on. How many people are now on the bus?
- A mother went to the market with her two children. They bought 24 oranges. They looked so delicious and all three of them ate one orange right away. On their way home, the children met a friend and all three children ate another orange. How many oranges were in the mother's basket when they got home?
- A father was working in the garden during the fall. He found a hole with 5 nuts in a tree, later he found 6 nuts buried in the ground, and then he found 8 nuts on a shelf in the garden shed. How many nuts were there in total?

Practice book. In second grade, it is good for the children to keep a practice book. What has been done through movement exercises can now be written down. A practice book is very handy and helps the children learn how to organize their work. The work in this practice book should still be done neatly.

Second Grade Math

Math Main Lesson Block #1: Place Value and the Times Tables

New material and content
- *The times tables.*
  - In this first math block of second grade, we begin to introduce the times and division tables.
  - Keep in mind that the goal is that by the end of the year, the class should be comfortable with all of the times tables from 1-12. This requires daily systematic work, and much careful planning.
  - Be sure to read *A Step-by-Step Progression for the Arithmetic Facts* (in the appendix).
- *Place value.* It is best to work with images when introducing place value.
  - *Gnomes and gems.* We can create a story about a community of gnomes who are miners of gems. They need to find a way to keep track of the gems and count them. It may be good for the students to try first to come up with a system on their own. One idea is as follows: Groups of 10 gems are put into small pouches. Groups of 10 pouches are put into small buckets. Groups of 10 buckets are put into wheel barrels, etc. In this way, the number 3,785 is represented by 3 wheel barrels, 7 buckets, 8 pouches, and 5 (single) gems. This is a nice story to illustrate in a main lesson book. It can lead into the next (perhaps less elaborate) story…
  - *A woodcutter's mill.* A woodcutter has a lumber mill that produces boards for sale in the village. Groups of 10 boards get tied into bundles. Groups of 10 bundles get put into crates. Groups of 10 crates get put onto horse wagons. In this way, the number 2,497 is represented by two wagons, 4 crates, 9 bundles, seven (single) boards. This story nicely lends itself to the children practicing place value by using craft (popsicle) sticks, which are available in most craft stores. You can simply give the students a large number of sticks, maybe around 2,400 sticks, and have the students group them like the woodcutter so they can count all of the sticks.
  - After the introduction of place value, number dictations can help the students practice with these newly discovered larger numbers.
- *The four processes.* Develop strategies for addition and subtraction. The students should be fluent with sums up to 24, and at ease up to 100. This work will continue throughout second grade.

Movement
- *The circle of twelve.* All of the times tables can also come out of a 12-circle. We like to introduce the circle of twelve because twelve represents a cosmic reality. The children are still very connected to the cosmos, the world they come from. The students will recognize the twelve in the clock, and in the twelve months (second block). We can do this for all of the times tables (starting with the two's times table). For example, consider the five's table. The children sit on chairs in a circle, representing the numbers of the clock. Another child stands in the center of the circle with a ball of yarn. The child representing the number 12 (which is also zero) holds one end of the yarn. The child in the center takes 5 steps and ends up at the number 5. This child takes the string and everyone says: "five equals one times five." In this way, the middle child passes through the numbers of the five's times all the way up to 60=12x5. The yarn went around the circle several times. Once this is completed, we have woven together a beautiful 12-pointed star.

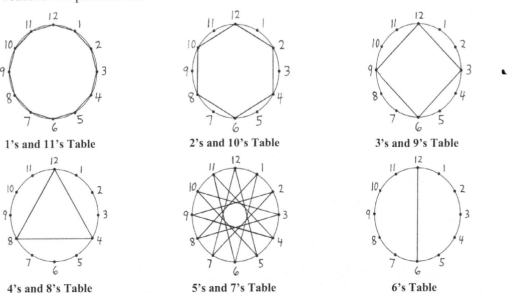

1's and 11's Table   2's and 10's Table   3's and 9's Table

4's and 8's Table   5's and 7's Table   6's Table

Second Grade Math

- *The circle of ten* [28]
    - The whole above process (just described with the 12-circle) can also be done with the 10-circle. In this case, we start with a 10-pointed circle, where each child on the circle represents the digits zero through nine. The pattern we now get with the yarn follows the last digit of the chosen times table.
    - For example, using the four's table, the yarn is passed from the 4 (**4**=1x4), to the 8 (**8**=2x4), to the 2 (because in this third step, 1**2**=3x4, which has 2 as a last digit), to the 6 (1**6**=4x4), to the 0 (2**0**=5x4), and then the digits repeat so the yarn revisits the same five children: 2**4**=6x4; 2**8**=7x4; 3**2**=8x4; 3**6**=9x4; 4**0**=10x4; 4**4**=11x4; and finally 4**8**=12x4. We have created a five-pointed star, which keeps repeating, again and again, no matter how far we choose to go – even if we went up to 100=25x4 we would get five 5-pointed stars laid on top of one another!

1's and 9's Table   2's and 8's Table   3's and 7's Table   4's and 6's Table   5's Table

- Why do the four's and six's tables produce the same geometrical pattern? Because they have similar qualities! The last digit for the four's table cycles every five steps (4,8,2,6,0), and the six's table has the same cycle, but backwards (6,2,8,4,0). In the same way, the one's table, the nine's table, and the eleven's table all produce the same 10-sided figure (decagon); the two's table, the eight's table, and the twelve's table all produce pentagons; and the three's table, and the seven's table both produce beautiful 10-pointed stars.
- Of course, all of this can be quite an amazing discovery for the second grader! They will come to the realization that for any two numbers that add to ten, their tables will produce the same geometric pattern, but it is produced backwards. This is because the last digits in their tables follow the same pattern.
- *Stepping.* Start at any given number between 100 and 1000 and have the whole class count forward and backward. Then do this in small groups and individually.
- *Clapping and stamping – Important!* Practice times tables with clapping and stamping in a rhythmical way. For example, using the four's times table: *four* (clap hands) *is* (two hands on upper legs) *one* (clap hands) *times* (arms crossed) *four* (clap hands). There are many possibilities!
- *More ideas for movement.* For more movement ideas see Henning Andersen's book, *Active Arithmetic*.

<u>Working with manipulatives</u>

- Manipulatives should be used less frequently in second grade than in first grade, but likely there are a few children who will still need the manipulatives (e.g., a string with beads).
- The number line at the wall in the class can be used for games, etc. We can ask questions like: Where is the number that is 5 more than 26?
- Board games can be fun, and some games with dice can help practice mental arithmetic. (See the appendix for a list of games for lower school math.)

<u>Bookwork</u>

- The beautiful geometrical forms we created during our movement exercises (with either the 12-circle or the 10-circle) can now be drawn into the children's main lesson books.
- Be sure to visit our website (**www.JamieYorkPress.com**) to see full-color pages from students' main lesson books.

---

[28] We are presenting two options (the 12-circle and the 10-circle) for working with the times tables within a circle. We encourage the teacher to choose one option or the other. Doing both circles in second grade is not recommended because it would be confusing to the students.

Second Grade Math

Math Main Lesson Block #2: Time

<u>New material and content</u>
- *Time orientation.* The main focus in this block is time: the days of the week, the months, and the clock. The children learn to read a clock with hands, where the minute hand is straight up on the 12, such as 4 o'clock, etc. We add the minutes in third grade.
- *The times and division tables.*
  - The goal is that by the end of the year, the class should be comfortable with all of the times and division tables from 1-12. This requires daily systematic work, and much careful planning.
  - Be sure to read *A Step-by-Step Progression for the Arithmetic Facts* (in the appendix).
- *The four processes.* We can slowly bring more difficult problems (but not too difficult!) to the children. Problems are presented both orally (with mental arithmetic) and in written form. Also, continue to develop strategies.
- *Place value.* We should review and further what was introduced in the first block.
- *Number dictations.* Number dictations should be done in order to help the students build an understanding of place value. With these number dictations we can vary the digits slightly, such as: 21, 12, 23, 32, 41, 14, 112, 121, 211, etc.
- *Making a calendar.* It may be best if this block falls in January, which is a perfect time for making calendars.
- In Christoph Jaffke's book, *Rhythms Rhymes Games and Songs for the Lower School*, one can find excellent poems for the theme of time and season.
- *Don't forget to review and practice!* Previously introduced material needs to be reviewed, practiced, and furthered. (See above *Practice and review of old material* under *Lessons and Topics for Second Grade Math*.)

<u>Movement</u>
- *Movement exercises for the times tables.* Continue to find interesting movement exercises for the times tables that use rhythm sticks, beanbags, and more.
- *Movement exercises for place value.* The class teacher can find and invent a variety of games that practice place value.
- *Moving the four processes on the number line.* For example, if you start at 38, and step forward by ten, where do you end up? And then, if you take another step? We can also do this with subtraction. This can also be helpful to develop strategies. For example, instead of stepping forward by 13, we first could take a step of ten followed by a step of three.
- *Moving with the clock.* The clock can be visualized by making the circle with 12 students and the hour hand and minute hand can be two different students.
- *Moving with the weeks and months.* We walk the days of the week and the months of the year forward and backwards with the class, in small groups, and individually.

<u>Working with manipulatives</u>
- *Making a clock.* The students can make a cardboard clock themselves, and then practice with it.

<u>Bookwork</u>
- The students continue to put the times and division tables in their main lesson books in an artistic way.
- *Pictures of time.* At 6 o'clock (morning) the sun comes up and we have breakfast; at 10 o'clock we have snack; at 12 o'clock (noon) the sun is overhead and we have lunch; at 6 o'clock the sun is setting as we eat, etc The students can draw all of these pictures beautifully in their main lesson books.
- The students can make a calendar with one page for each month. We can provide them with a pre-printed grid, which they can glue to a piece of paper. Every page has a poem of the month, and also has a drawing and includes the birthdays of their classmates.
- Be sure to visit our website (**www.JamieYorkPress.com**) to see full-color pages from students' main lesson books.

Second Grade Math

Math Main Lesson Block #3: Bringing it all together!

<u>New material and content</u>
- The major purpose of this main lesson block is to bring everything together that has been introduced previously. Of course, it is always best to find new variations to previously introduced material. New games (see the appendix for a list of games for lower school math), riddles and/or puzzles can be added.
- *The times tables.*
  - Finish the times and division tables up to 12 in an artistic way.
  - Keep in mind that the goal is that by the end of the year, the class should be comfortable with all of the times tables from 1-12 in a row. This requires daily systematic work, and much careful planning.
  - Be sure to read *A Step-by-Step Progression for the Arithmetic Facts* (in the appendix).
  - The children should create a times table square soon after all of the tables (1 through 12) have been introduced. This square should be done beautifully, with nice colors. The children can then try to find hidden secrets and patterns in the times table square.
- *The four processes.*
  - We continue to work with the four processes.
  - Ensure that the concepts of multiplication and division are clear.
- *Don't forget to review and practice!* Previously introduced material needs to be reviewed, practiced, and furthered. (See above *Practice and review of old material under Lessons and Topics for Second Grade Math.*)

<u>Movement</u>
- *Rhythmical exercises.* We should continue with daily rhythmical exercises, but we can now do more complicated movements for the times tables, and bring many variations.
- For example, we could clap on the numbers that are in the two's times table, and, at the same time, stamp our feet on the numbers that are in the three's times table. All of this happens while we speak the numbers sequentially. (See below, where "c" = clap, and "s" = stamp.) We can also use different percussion instruments.

1	2	3	4	5	6	7	8	9	10	11	12	13	14	15	16
	c	s	c		cs		c	s	c		cs		c	s	c

<u>Working with manipulatives</u>
- Manipulatives are used less and less frequently. (See *Regarding number lines and manipulatives* under *The art of teaching math* above.)

<u>Bookwork</u>
- The children should finish their work with the times tables in their main lesson books.
- The children can now put the *times table square* into their book. In many ways, this is the culmination of all of our work through the year with the times tables. It should be done very beautifully!
- Be sure to visit our website (**www.JamieYorkPress.com**) to see full-color pages from students' main lesson books.

Second Grade Math

More Ideas for Teaching Second Grade Math
(Be sure to reread the section, *Thoughts on Teaching Math in the Lower Grades*, found at the start of this book.)

Commutative property. Years ago, schools taught the commutative property (e.g., 4x3 is the same as 3x4) and also the associative property – both in a very abstract way. There is, of course, no real reason to have the children become familiar with these terms, but we do want to look for opportunities for the children to discover the principles behind this. For the children, 5x3 (i.e., five groups of three) is a very different process than 3x5 (i.e., three groups of five). Likewise, 2+6 is a different process than 6+2, yet both yield the same sum. This can be an exciting "aha" moment for the children when they discover for themselves that the two numbers being multiplied or added can be switched and the result will be the same.

Different kinds of subtraction
- *Three ways of looking at minus*. There are (at least) three ways to look at a subtraction problem. (This is for the teacher to keep in mind; the students may not be fully conscious of this until 3rd grade.) Using the example of 20 – 13:
    - *As a Take Away (or Subtraction) problem*. We take away 13 from 20.
    - *As a Difference Problem*. We ask ourselves: "How far apart are 13 and 20?" or "How many steps are there going from 13 to 20?" This will be especially clear to the students once they have moved it on the number line.
    - *As the Reverse of Addition*. We ask ourselves: "13 plus what is 20?"
- The goal is to develop flexibility in the children's thinking, so that sometimes they look at it as a *difference* problem, and sometimes as a *take away* problem, depending upon which approach is easier for a given problem.
- The teacher should try to be consistent in the use of the words "take away", "difference", "subtract", etc. By saying "26 minus 14", we leave it open for the children to solve the problem by either *taking away* or *finding the difference*.
- The students should still be doing subtraction predominantly in the horizontal form (and in mental arithmetic) well into third grade, and beyond.

No "carrying" or "borrowing" yet. It is best to delay vertical addition and subtraction until third grade. (See above, *Keep in the horizontal as much as possible* under *Developing a Sense of Number/Topics in the math classroom*.)

Second Grade Math

A step-by-step progression for addition in second grade

Notes:
- Of course, there are more steps possible than are listed below. This is intended to give the teacher some possible ideas of what could be done to work in a structured way.
- Important: remember that this is all "mental arithmetic". Vertical addition isn't introduced until third grade.
- Because these problems aren't done using vertical addition (i.e., carrying), this all lends itself to developing strategies. For example, after we have done quite a bit of this work, imagine all of the ways that a student could figure out 46+19?
- The answer doesn't always have to appear at the end of the problem; it is important to vary the presentation of these problems, so that the students are flexible. For example, instead of $29 + 6 = \_\_$, we could write it as $29 + \_\_ = 35$.
- It is important to find "the story" behind a problem, or to "translate" the problem into spoken language. For example, with $7 + \_\_ = 12$, I ask myself, "How much do I need to add to 7 in order to get 12?" or "Seven plus what makes twelve?", or "What is the difference between 12 and 7?"

Step #1: Adding multiples of 10.

$10 + 10 = \_\_ \rightarrow 20 = 10 + \_\_$
$20 + 10 = \_\_ \rightarrow 30 = 20 + \_\_$
$30 + 10 = \_\_$ etc.
$20 + 20 = \_\_ \rightarrow 40 = 20 + \_\_$
$30 + 20 = \_\_ \rightarrow 50 = 30 + \_\_$
$40 + 20 = \_\_$ etc.
$30 + 30 = \_\_ \rightarrow 60 = 30 + \_\_$
$40 + 30 = \_\_ \rightarrow 70 = 40 + \_\_$
$50 + 30 = \_\_$ etc.
etc.

Step #2: Two-digit plus one-digit (without carry).

$25 + 3 = \_\_ \rightarrow 28 = \_\_ + 3$
$36 + 2 = \_\_ \rightarrow 38 = \_\_ + 2$
$72 + 5 = \_\_ \rightarrow 77 = \_\_ + 5$
etc.

Step #3: Adding 10.

$25 + 10 = \_\_ \rightarrow 35 = \_\_ + 10$
$36 + 10 = \_\_ \rightarrow 46 = \_\_ + 10$
$58 + 10 = \_\_ \rightarrow 68 = \_\_ + 10$
etc.

Step #4: Two-digit plus a multiple of 10.

$25 + 30 = \_\_ \rightarrow 55 = \_\_ + 30$
$36 + 40 = \_\_ \rightarrow 76 = \_\_ + 40$
$58 + 20 = \_\_ \rightarrow 78 = \_\_ + 20$
etc.

Step #5: Two-digit number plus a number between 10 and 20 (without carrying).

$35 + 13 = \_\_ \rightarrow 48 = 35 + \_\_$
$74 + 12 = \_\_ \rightarrow 86 = 74 + \_\_$
$52 + 16 = \_\_ \rightarrow 68 = 52 + \_\_$
etc.

Step #6: Two-digit number plus a number between 10 and 20, and with ones digits adding to 10.

$44 + 16 = \_\_ \rightarrow 60 = 44 + \_\_$
$67 + 13 = \_\_ \rightarrow 80 = 67 + \_\_$
$63 + 17 = \_\_ \rightarrow 80 = 63 + \_\_$
$81 + 19 = \_\_ \rightarrow 100 = 81 + \_\_$
etc.

Step #7: Two-digit doubling.

$24 + 24 = \_\_ \rightarrow 48 = \_\_ + \_\_$
$32 + 32 = \_\_ \rightarrow 64 = \_\_ + \_\_$
$45 + 45 = \_\_ \rightarrow 90 = \_\_ + \_\_$
$49 + 49 = \_\_ \rightarrow 98 = \_\_ + \_\_$
etc.

Step #8: Adding any two 2-digit numbers. The big, challenging step!

$53 + 18 = \_\_ \rightarrow 71 = 53 + \_\_$
$43 + 19 = \_\_ \rightarrow 62 = 43 + \_\_$
$26 + 54 = \_\_ \rightarrow 80 = 26 + \_\_$
$48 + 34 = \_\_ \rightarrow 82 = 48 + \_\_$
etc.

Second Grade Math

A step-by-step progression for subtraction in second grade

Notes:
- Of course, there are more steps possible than are listed below. This is intended to give the teacher some possible ideas of what could be done to work in a structured way.
- Important: remember that this is all "mental arithmetic". Vertical subtraction isn't introduced until third grade.
- Because these problems aren't done using vertical subtraction, this all lends itself to developing strategies. For example, after we have done quite a bit of this work, imagine all of the ways that a student could figure out 42–15.
- The answer doesn't always have to appear at the end of the problem; it is important to vary the presentation of these problems, so that the students are flexible. For example, instead of $29 - 6 = \_\_$, we could write it as $29 - \_\_ = 23$, or $\_\_ - 6 = 23$.
- It is important to find "the story" behind a problem, or to "translate" the problem into spoken language. For example, with $17 = 22 - \_\_$, I can ask: "How many do I need to take away from 22 in order to get 17?"

Step #1: Subtracting multiples of 10.
$20 - 10 = \_\_ \rightarrow 10 = 20 - \_\_$
$70 - 30 = \_\_ \rightarrow 40 = 70 - \_\_$
$100 - 60 = \_\_ \rightarrow 40 = 100 - \_\_$
etc.

Step #2: Subtracting one-digit from two-digits (*without* regrouping).
$29 - 3 = \_\_ \rightarrow 26 = 29 - \_\_$
$35 - 4 = \_\_ \rightarrow 31 = 35 - \_\_$
$77 - 6 = \_\_ \rightarrow 71 = 77 - \_\_$
etc.

Step #3: Subtracting one-digit from two-digits (*with* regrouping).
$21 - 3 = \_\_ \rightarrow 18 = \_\_ - 3$
$35 - 8 = \_\_ \rightarrow 27 = \_\_ - 8$
$77 - 9 = \_\_ \rightarrow 68 = \_\_ - 9$
etc.

Step #4: Subtracting two 2-digit numbers resulting in a one-digit number, *part I*.
$29 - 23 = \_\_ \rightarrow 6 = 29 - \_\_$
$35 - 31 = \_\_ \rightarrow 4 = 35 - \_\_$
$77 - 72 = \_\_ \rightarrow 5 = 77 - \_\_$
etc.

Step #5: Subtracting two 2-digit numbers resulting in a one-digit number, *part II*.
$33 - 26 = \_\_ \rightarrow 7 = 33 - \_\_$
$44 - 38 = \_\_ \rightarrow 6 = 44 - \_\_$
$77 - 68 = \_\_ \rightarrow 9 = 77 - \_\_$
etc.

Step #6: Subtracting multiples of ten.
$33 - 10 = \_\_ \rightarrow 23 = 33 - \_\_$
$59 - 20 = \_\_ \rightarrow 39 = 59 - \_\_$
$87 - 40 = \_\_ \rightarrow 47 = \_\_ - 40$
etc.

Step #7: Subtracting 11 to 19 *without* regrouping.
$48 - 15 = \_\_ \rightarrow 33 = 48 - \_\_$
$56 - 12 = \_\_ \rightarrow 44 = 56 - \_\_$
$97 - 16 = \_\_ \rightarrow 81 = 97 - \_\_$
etc.

Step #8: Subtracting 11 to 19 resulting in a multiple of ten.
$48 - 18 = \_\_ \rightarrow 30 = 48 - \_\_$
$56 - 16 = \_\_ \rightarrow 40 = 56 - \_\_$
$97 - 17 = \_\_ \rightarrow 80 = \_\_ - 17$
etc.

Step #9: Subtracting 11 to 19 *with* regrouping – developing strategies!
$53 - 18 = \_\_ \rightarrow 35 = 53 - \_\_$
(perhaps do 53–10–3–5, or 53–20+2)
$82 - 14 = \_\_ \rightarrow 68 = 82 - \_\_$
$47 - 18 = \_\_ \rightarrow 29 = 47 - \_\_$
etc.

Step #10: Subtracting any two 2-digit numbers. The hardest problems!
$53 - 38 = \_\_ \rightarrow 15 = 53 - \_\_$
$63 - 28 = \_\_ \rightarrow 35 = 63 - \_\_$
$87 - 38 = \_\_ \rightarrow 49 = 87 - \_\_$
etc.

—Third Grade Math—

Overview of Child Development in Third Grade

The golden years come to an end as the child steps out of his little kingdom. This is the 9/10-year change, which usually comes towards the end of third grade. To the child, this can feel like a terrible loss and make him insecure. This is accompanied by a separation between the child and the world around him. He can also feel that his teacher has changed. The child may become lonely, insecure, and critical.

To help the children with this phase of their development we study the Old Testament. The lawfulness and lessons from the stories of the Hebrew people help to make the child feel more secure inwardly. Main lesson blocks like farming and house building help the child to develop a new relationship with the world around him.

The eagerness to learn is still strong; this is a time of real blossoming. With the sturdy foundation of the first two grades, the children can apply their mathematical knowledge to practical, everyday situations. Once the students have the feeling that they are nourished, they become less anxious about stepping into this new phase of their life. For the teaching of math, this means that we can bring them measurement and vertical arithmetic
(e.g., carrying, long division, etc.). Having the children learn the arithmetic facts by heart is perhaps our most important goal.

Curriculum Summary for Third Grade Math

The world of numbers
- The number world becomes fluent up to 1000 and at ease with the numbers up into the millions.
- Number dictations should be continued in third grade.
- Place value work should be continued from second grade, but now with larger numbers.

Learning all of the Arithmetic Facts!! **Very important!**
- Now is the time to learn the multiplication and division facts (that come from these tables) out of order. The groundwork was set in second grade, when the children learned their times/division tables (1-12). Also, all of the addition and subtraction facts are reviewed and strengthened.
- See *All about the Third Grade Arithmetic Facts Practice Sheets* (under *More Ideas for Teaching Third Grade Math*), and *A Step-by-Step Progression for the Arithmetic Facts* (in the appendix).

The four processes: Working vertically. Before third grade, the children have only been working with problems written horizontally.
- *Vertical addition*. This is the first experience with working vertically. Slowly, build up to adding two 4-digit numbers. Vertical addition problems may be practiced extensively.
- *Vertical subtraction*. Perhaps, less time is spent here than on vertical addition. Don't make it too complicated; much more vertical subtraction practice will be done in fourth grade.
- *Vertical multiplication*. As with vertical subtraction, this could be just an introduction. In third grade, vertical multiplication should be limited to single digit multipliers (i.e., 2347 x 5 might be the hardest). Don't overdo it! Two-digit multipliers should wait until fourth grade.
- *Vertical division* (long division).
  - Third grade or fourth grade? Vertical division (i.e., long division) is a very complicated procedure for many children. It requires division with remainders, multiplication, and subtraction. It requires that the children are fluent with their times/division tables. It requires the students to be systematic and organized in their work. For all of these reasons, each teacher needs to carefully consider whether the class is truly ready to be introduced to vertical division at the end of third grade. Most likely, it is best to wait until fourth grade.
  - If vertical division is introduced in third grade, then the division problems should be limited to two-step problems (e.g., 152 ÷ 4 = 38) that have divisors between 1 and 12. Keep it simple!

The four processes: Working horizontally. Even though the children are being introduced to working with the four processes in vertical form, the bulk of their work with the four processes is still in horizontal form – as given on their *arithmetic facts practice sheets*. We should begin practicing horizontal division problems that result in a remainder (e.g., 46÷7).

Third Grade Math

Measurement
- This is a fun, hands-on block!
- In this main lesson, we introduce time, distance, weight and volume.
- Additionally, bartering and the use of money is handled in a simple and practical way.
- Estimation is also an important part of this block.

Recommended Reading for Third Grade Math

- Henning Anderson, *Active Arithmetic*. AWSNA Publications.
- Herman von Baravalle, *The Teaching Of Arithmetic And The Waldorf School Plan*. Waldorf School Monographs, 1967, third edition.
- Else Gottgens, Joyful Recognition.
- Else Gottgens, Waldorf Education in Practice.
- Dorothy Harrer, *Math Lessons For Elementary Grades*. AWSNA Publications.
- Christoph Jaffke, *Rhythms, Rhymes, Games and Songs for the Lower School*. Published by the Pedagogische Forschung Stelle, Der Bund der Freien Waldorf Schule in Stuttgart.
- Lipping Ma, *Knowing and Teaching Elementary Mathematics*. Lawrence Erlbaum Assoc. Publishers 1919, London.
- Ernst Schuberth, *Teaching Mathematics for First and Second Grades in Waldorf Schools*. Rudolf Steiner College Press. (Especially the section about math weaknesses, pages 59 and up.)
- John A. van de Walle, *Elementary and Middle School Mathematics*. Virginia Commonwealth University, Longman, NY.

Lessons and Topics for Third Grade Math

Scheduling

The curriculum calls again for twelve weeks of math (three main lesson blocks of four weeks each), with one week of review at the end of the school year.

Don't forget!!

- *Every day*, we should review the previous day's lesson.
- *Every day*, we should bring something new to the children.
- *Every day*, the students should practice the new material and selected review topics.

Practice and review (of old material)

- Most of the topics listed below were introduced some time ago. In order for the children to learn a topic well, it needs to be systematically reviewed. Obviously, all previous topics cannot be reviewed every day. The teacher needs to decide which topics are the most important to review each day. Some of these topics may need to be reviewed and practiced nearly every day, whether the class is in a math block, or not. As a general guideline, the class should practice 30 minutes daily, when in a math block, and about 10 minutes daily (in the morning) when not in a math block. (Also see *Review and Practice* under *Principles of Waldorf Education* above.)

Third Grade Math

<u>Daily practice sheets</u>. *Learning the arithmetic facts by heart.*
- The groundwork was set in second grade when the children learned their times/division tables (1-12) in a row. They must now learn the multiplication and division facts (that come from these tables) out of order, as well as all of the addition facts and subtraction facts.
- Remember that multiplication and division always go together. If we are working with a particular multiplication fact (e.g., 7x4=28) then we are working with the corresponding division fact (e.g., 28÷4=7 and 28÷7=4) at the same time. Additionally, facts should also be practiced in a variety of different ways, such as 7x__=28, and __÷4=7.
- Be sure to read *All about the Third Grade Arithmetic Facts Practice Sheets under More Ideas for Teaching Third Grade Math* below. Also read *A step-by-step progression for the arithmetic facts* in the appendix.

<u>The times/division tables</u>
- *Movement.* Look at our example in second grade, where we did the times table of two (with a clap) and three (with a stamp) while we counted. Now, we can add nodding our heads with the four's times table. Henning Anderson gives several other good examples.
- Every time we do a times table with movement exercises, we should also find a way of writing it into our main lesson books in a way that shows the relationships.

<u>Practice with the four processes</u>
- Even though the children in third grade are being introduced to vertical arithmetic, they still should practice horizontal arithmetic (e.g., with their daily practice sheets). It is also important to keep up daily mental arithmetic (through eighth grade!). All of this helps ensure that their sense of number continues to develop and that they strengthen their ability to do simple calculations in their head.
- We should continue to encourage the children to find strategies when working with the four processes.
- We should begin to practice simple division problems that result in a remainder (e.g., 46÷7).

<u>Mental arithmetic</u>
- Practice mental arithmetic daily (for 10 minutes or less), and continue to develop strategies through this work.
- Work up to calculations like 46 + 5; 28 + 31; 75 – 68; 73 – 4; 24 ÷ 4; 100 – 13; 51= 46 + __.
- *Halfway problems.* These problems should start off easy in second grade, and now, in third grade, can get a bit more challenging. Some examples are:
  - What number is halfway between 25 and 41?
  - What number is halfway between 25 and 61?
  - What number is halfway between 250 and 450?

<u>Word Problems</u>. Simple puzzles, riddles, and games can be valuable at this age. (See *A list of Games* in the appendix.)

<u>Reading clocks</u>. In second grade, the students were introduced to reading clocks (with hands), at least as far as reading times like 4 o'clock, 7 o'clock, etc. (where the minute hand is up at 12). Now, in third grade, we learn to read all possible times, such as 5:23, 11:04, etc. We also cover the following: 4:30 is the same as "half-past four"; 8:45 is "quarter to nine"; 10:50 is "ten to eleven"; and 7:25 is about "half-past seven".

<u>Practice book</u>. In second grade, the children began to keep a practice book, which should be continued in third grade and beyond. As always, the work in a practice book should be done neatly. In third grade it teaches the children how to organize their work.

<u>The world of numbers</u>. We review counting up to 1000, and beyond, forward and backward. Number dictations should also be continued.

Third Grade Math

Math Main Lesson Block #1: Vertical Addition and Subtraction

New material and content
- *Vertical addition and subtraction* (a.k.a., "carrying and borrowing"). This is a new (and exciting!) subject.
  - This is just an introduction to vertical addition and subtraction. Over the course of the third grade year, we will build up to adding two 4-digit numbers (e.g., 8364+8375) and subtracting two 3-digit numbers (e.g., 643–387).
  - *Terminology.* Try not to use the word "borrowing" with the students because we never actually give anything back in the process.[29] We will not use "borrowing", but instead, we will call the whole procedure "vertical subtraction", and the strategy that gets us around the tricky situation (where, in a given column, the top digit is smaller than the bottom digit) we will call "regrouping".
  - The students first need to be confident with place value. Therefore, a strong review of second grade place value will be necessary.
  - It is wise to also review the regrouping of numbers.
    - For example, how can we regroup 53 as the sum of two numbers? It could be written as $53 = 50+3$, or $53 = 40+13$, or $53 = 30+23$, or $53 = 52+1$, or $53 = 48+5$, etc.
  - Be sure to read *A step-by-step progression for vertical addition and subtraction* under *More Ideas for Teaching Third Grade Math* below.
- *Don't forget to review and practice!* Previously introduced material needs to be reviewed, practiced, and furthered. (See above *Practice and review of old material* under *Lessons and Topics for Third Grade Math*.)

Movement
- The times tables should now be done with more challenging movement. Different times tables could be "moved" at the same time.
  - *Example*: We can clap the two, stamp the three, and move your head on the six.
  - *Example*: With the 3, 6, 9, and 12 tables, have one student count, perhaps by beating a drum, and assign the rest of the class different tables (3, 6, 9, 12). Different movements are assigned to each table. Perhaps the phlegmatics should have the 3's table, so that they move the most.
  - After doing such exercises, we should ask the class some questions, such as: When did we all move at the same time? When did only the nines move? When was there no movement? etc.
  - Try to find many more ways of bringing movement to the times tables so that the class can work together in a joyful way.

Working with manipulatives
- Students should now be able to imagine the regrouping of the numbers, therefore manipulatives should be avoided.

Bookwork
- The students should add many vertical addition and subtraction problems into their books.
- The work needs to be neat and orderly!! Use appropriate colors (e.g., green for adding, and blue for subtracting, etc.).
- Be sure to visit our website (**www.JamieYorkPress.com**) to see full-color pages from students' main lesson books.

---

[29] Lipping Ma, *Knowing and Teaching Elementary Mathematics*.

Third Grade Math

Math Main Lesson Block #2: Measurement

New material and content
- *Measurement.* This is the main theme of the main lesson.
  - *Linear measurement.*
    - The children are introduced to linear measurement through hands-on experiences based on the human body.
    - They should measure things in and around the classroom.
    - As a class we can make a simple graph that shows one particular student's height over a period of several months – or maybe each child could do that for himself at home.
  - *Weight.* Weight should also be part of the experience. The students can weigh objects in the classroom, and they can weigh one another.
  - *Volume and liquid measure.* With liquid measure we should pour cups into gallons, tablespoons into a cup, etc.
  - *Origins.* The historical origins of the various units of measurement can be brought in an imaginative way (e.g., through the story of Noah's Ark).
  - *Practical use.* Of course, it is best to show practical uses of measurement, such as with simple building projects, cooking recipes, etc.
  - *Estimation.* The students should practice estimating. For example, they could estimate the length of a board, the height of a tree, the distance between two rocks, the weight of an animal. We should always try to estimate before taking an actual measurement.
  - *Unit conversions.* The students should practice very simple unit conversions, such as converting feet to yards, feet to inches, pints to quarts, etc.
- *Money.* This is also the time to introduce the children to our currency. They can make their own money (coins and bills) and stock a store, or even create a market place. We can also create games for money. Through all of this activity, the children practice counting money and making change.
- *Vertical addition and subtraction.* Vertical addition and subtraction was introduced in the first math block of third grade. In the meantime, this new material has been "put to sleep" (see *The conscious use of forgetting* under *Principles of Waldorf Education* above). It is important that we not touch upon new material in between two math blocks. Now that the material (vertical addition and subtraction) has had its proper "rest", we can review it and then deepen it.
- *Division with remainders.* This should be done using the same dividend but different divisors. For example, using the number 14, divide it by 1, 2, 3, etc. (14÷1 = __ ; 14÷2 = __; 14÷3 = __; 14÷4 = __, etc.) After some time, the students will improve at figuring out the remainder. This is preparation for vertical (long) division.
- *Don't forget to review and practice!* Previously introduced material needs to be reviewed, practiced, and furthered. (See above *Practice and review of old material* under *Lessons and Topics for Third Grade Math.*)

Movement. Continue the movement activities that were done in the first block.

Working with manipulatives
- Of course, there are unlimited possibilities for hands-on experiences and activities during this measurement block. This should bring a lively spirit to the lessons and enthuse the students.
- Many props and visual aids are helpful for this block. For example, with volumes we could use milk cartons, jugs, bottles, spoons, cups, cans, etc.
- Our work with money and currency lends itself nicely to working with manipulatives.

Bookwork
- The children should write what they have experienced (e.g., one gallon is 4 quarts, etc.) in their main lesson books. They can make drawings (e.g., of a foot) as it applies to the units of measurement.
- Be sure to visit our website (**www.JamieYorkPress.com**) to see full-color pages from students' main lesson books.

Third Grade Math

Math Main Lesson Block #3: Vertical Multiplication (and Division?)

<u>New material and content</u>
- *Vertical multiplication.*
  - Vertical multiplication can only be successful when the students feel confident with the times tables.
  - In third grade, vertical multiplication should be limited to single digit multipliers (i.e., 2347 x 5 might be the hardest). Don't overdo it! Two-digit multipliers should wait until fourth grade.
  - Be sure to read *A step-by-step progression for vertical multiplication* under *More Ideas for Teaching Third Grade Math* below.
- *Vertical (long) division.*
  - Every teacher needs to carefully consider whether the class is truly ready to be introduced to vertical division at the end of third grade, or whether it is best to wait until fourth grade.
  - If it is decided to introduce vertical division at the end of third grade, then keep these things in mind:
    - *Keep it simple!* The problems should be limited to two-step problems (e.g., $152 \div 4 = 38$) having divisors between 1 and 12.
    - *Keep it brief!* Be sure that the class doesn't get overwhelmed with too many vertical division problems. A brief introduction should be enough.
    - *Be sure to read* the sections on vertical division found in the fourth grade chapter of this book, including:
      - *Working vertically (division)* under *Lessons and Topics for Fourth Grade Math* (at the beginning of the fourth grade chapter).
      - *A step-by-step progression for vertical division* under *More Ideas for Teaching Fourth Grade Math* (at the end of the fourth grade chapter).
- *Don't forget to review and practice!* Previously introduced material needs to be reviewed, practiced, and furthered. (See above *Practice and review of old material* under *Lessons and Topics for Third Grade Math*.)

<u>Movement</u>
- It is a challenging but important task to bring all the times tables together in movement. Here is one idea of how it could be done where the children are the workers on a ship:
  - The captain counts the ones; the twos are sweeping the deck; the threes throw the buckets of water on the deck; the fours raise the sails; the fives pull up the anchor, etc.
  - Groups move and speak when they hear a number from their times table.
  - It is fine if some students only observe, since there are several questions that can be asked at the end of the exercise (e.g., When did we hear only the captain? When was the whole crew moving and speaking?, etc.).

<u>Working with manipulatives</u>
- We recommend keeping away from manipulatives during this vertical multiplication main lesson. The students need to internalize the processes.

<u>Bookwork</u>
- The children can include several examples (some with all of the steps) of vertical multiplication (and vertical division?) in their main lesson book.
- Be sure to visit our website (**www.JamieYorkPress.com**) to see full-color pages from students' main lesson books.

Third Grade Math

More Ideas for Teaching Third Grade Math
(Be sure to reread the section, *Thoughts on Teaching Math in the Lower Grades* found at the start of this book.)

A step-by-step progression for vertical addition and subtraction

Step #1: Two-digit addition/subtraction without carrying or borrowing. (Many of these problems should be done during the first math block of third grade.)

$$\begin{array}{rcl} 35 & \rightarrow & 30+5 \\ +14 & \rightarrow & +(10+4) \\ \hline 49 & \leftarrow & 40+9 \end{array} \qquad \begin{array}{rcl} 56 & \rightarrow & 50+6 \\ -23 & \rightarrow & -(20+3) \\ \hline 33 & \leftarrow & 30+3 \end{array}$$

Step #2: Using and showing regrouping strategies. (Many of these problems should be done during the first math block of third grade.)

$$\begin{array}{rcl} 46 & \rightarrow & 40+6 \\ +38 & \rightarrow & +(30+8) \\ \hline 84 & \leftarrow & 70+14 \end{array} \qquad \begin{array}{rcl} 83 & \rightarrow & 70+13 \\ -25 & \rightarrow & -(20+5) \\ \hline 58 & \leftarrow & 50+8 \end{array}$$

Note: It is important that the children have worked a good deal with regrouping strategies (but not with vertical arithmetic) beginning in second grade.

Step #3: The short cut – standard, vertical addition and subtraction. (Many of these problems should be done during the second math block of third grade.)

Using the same examples as above:

$$\begin{array}{r} \overset{1}{}46 \\ +38 \\ \hline 84 \end{array} \qquad \begin{array}{r} {}^7\!\!\not{8}^{1}3 \\ -25 \\ \hline 58 \end{array}$$

Notes:
- In order to make these problems more meaningful, try creating problems that relate to various activities.
- It is best to introduce vertical addition and subtraction in an artistic way. For example:
  - With vertical addition, we can draw a house where there is a level for every number.
  - The answer ends up in the basement, and the attic is used for the "carry" numbers.
  - This should not be too elaborate of a story; it is simply an artistic way of writing it down.
  - Something similar can also be done for vertical subtraction.
- Visit our website **www.JamieYorkPress.com** to see full-color drawings of all of this.

Third Grade Math

A step-by-step progression for vertical multiplication (with single-digit multipliers)

Step #1: Write down familiar multiplication facts in vertical form.

$$\begin{array}{r} 4 \\ \times 7 \\ \hline 28 \end{array}$$

Step #2: A 2-digit number (in expanded form) times a single-digit number.

$$\begin{array}{r} 24 \\ \times 6 \\ \end{array} \rightarrow \begin{array}{r} 20 + 4 \\ \times 6 \\ \hline 24 \\ +120 \\ \hline 144 \end{array} \quad \text{(The 2-digit number is regrouped.)}$$

Step #3: The short cut – standard, vertical multiplication (again, 2-digit times 1-digit).

$$\begin{array}{r} \overset{2}{} \\ 24 \\ \times 6 \\ \hline 144 \end{array}$$

Step #4: A 3-digit number (in expanded form) times a single-digit number.

$$\begin{array}{r} 486 \\ \times 3 \\ \end{array} \rightarrow \begin{array}{r} 400 + 80 + 6 \\ \times 3 \\ \hline 18 \\ 240 \\ +1200 \\ \hline 1458 \end{array}$$

Step #5: The short cut – standard, vertical multiplication (again, 3-digit times 1-digit).

$$\begin{array}{r} {}^{2\,1} \\ 486 \\ \times 3 \\ \hline 1458 \end{array}$$

Step #6: Don't write down the carry digit!

$$\begin{array}{r} 486 \\ \times 3 \\ \hline 1458 \end{array}$$

It is important for the students to work towards not writing down the carry digit (i.e., holding the carry digit in their head).

All about the *Third Grade Arithmetic Facts Practice* Sheets

- Free download!! You can download our *third grade arithmetic facts practice sheets* for free from our website: **www.JamieYorkPress.com**.
- Facts of the Week! (See next page.) The central idea of these sheets is that there are five facts of the week written on the board, which the teacher works on with the whole class during the week in a variety of ways (e.g., using movement, rhythmical work, games, etc.). These facts of the week then appear multiple times on the sheets for the current week, and are then reviewed systematically for the next several weeks.
- Background work. These sheets should ideally be the culmination of two years of work. If the work in first and second grade has been effective, then the children should feel that these sheets are easy. If these sheets become too difficult and tedious, then it is likely that the classroom work being done in preparation for these sheets is either insufficient or not effective enough.
- Timing and rhythm. The intention is that the first "third grade arithmetic facts" practice sheet should be done at some point between the end of September and the end of October in third grade. It can, of course, vary depending upon the class. After that, a sheet should be done (nearly) every day until the whole set of 100 sheets is completed. There are 20 weeks (100 days) of sheets in this set. Each sheet has 30 problems.
- Completion. Since these sheets are designed to be an integral part of learning the math facts, it is important that each sheet of the entire set be completed, otherwise certain facts won't get adequate exposure.
- Caution! This should be fun and easy for the students. If successful, this builds their confidence. It is important to make sure that these sheets don't become torture for the students. Try to de-emphasize the importance of speed. Help the students to realize that improvement is what is important.
- The whole picture. The 30 problems listed on a particular sheet are only a part of the daily math practice. **It would be very unfortunate if daily math practice consisted of nothing more than the 30 arithmetic facts practice problems that appear on these sheets.**
    - When the class *is not* in a math main lesson, daily math practice should take about 10 minutes. The 30 arithmetic facts may take 3-5 minutes. The remaining 5-7 minutes can be spent doing a few written (vertical) arithmetic problems, some brief rhythmical work, or something else.
    - When the class *is* in a math main lesson, daily math practice should take about 30 minutes. The 30 arithmetic facts may take 3-5 minutes. After that, the remaining 25 minutes of math practice (during a math main lesson) consists of the material that was brought in previous blocks and the current block.
- The elements of math practice. The following list shows some of the aspects to consider when planning math practice for the day.
    - *Arithmetic facts practice sheet*. The teacher copies by hand the 30 problems from our *Third Grade Arithmetic Facts Practice Sheets* onto paper to be photocopied.[30] (about 5 minutes)
    - *Mental arithmetic*. The teacher may decide to read the first 6 problems out loud.
    - *Extra math practice problems*. There should be a few extra problems that the teacher comes up with and writes on the board. The students copy them into their practice books and work out the answers. These problems also include practice and review of material covered in previous math blocks. (Takes 20-25 minutes if the class is in a math block, otherwise only 5 minutes.)
    - *Challenge problems*. It is important that the last few problems (that the teacher adds on) be more challenging in order to keep the "quicker" students fully engaged.
- What comes next? The next set of practice sheets is titled *Fourth Grade Arithmetic Facts Review Sheets* and is intended to thoroughly review the math facts covered on the first practice sheets.
- The hope is that just five minutes per day of practicing these arithmetic facts results in the whole class quite effortlessly learning their math facts by heart.
- And what happens if…? We hope that it won't happen, but there may be a few children at the end of third grade who still haven't solidly learned their arithmetic facts. In order to help these children, we can give them a multiplication/division table (i.e., a square for the tables). Additionally, these students should study the basic arithmetic problems with flashcards during morning practice time.

---

[30] *Saving paper*. Try to find ways to reduce the amount of paper being used. For example, rather than using one sheet of paper each day, each side could be divided into three columns (i.e., 1 sheet = 6 days). This is one of many ways to help develop an environmental consciousness in the students.

The 105 Key Arithmetic Facts (each appears as a "fact of the week")

8 + 2	6 + 6	10 − 8	13 − 9	3 x 3	6 x 6
9 + 2	7 + 6	10 − 7	13 − 8	3 x 4	6 x 7
7 + 3	8 + 6	10 − 6	13 − 7	3 x 5	6 x 8
8 + 3	9 + 6	10 − 5	13 − 6	3 x 6	6 x 9
9 + 3	7 + 7	10 − 4	13 − 5	3 x 7	6 x 12
6 + 4	8 + 7	10 − 3	13 − 4	3 x 8	7 x 7
7 + 4	9 + 7	10 − 2	14 − 9	3 x 9	7 x 8
8 + 4	8 + 8	11 − 9	14 − 8	3 x 12	7 x 9
9 + 4	9 + 8	11 − 8	14 − 7	4 x 4	7 x 12
5 + 5	9 + 9	11 − 7	14 − 6	4 x 5	8 x 8
6 + 5		11 − 6	14 − 5	4 x 6	8 x 9
7 + 5		11 − 5	15 − 9	4 x 7	8 x 12
8 + 5		11 − 4	15 − 8	4 x 8	9 x 9
9 + 5		11 − 3	15 − 7	4 x 9	9 x 12
		11 − 2	15 − 6	4 x 12	11 x 11
		12 − 9	16 − 9	5 x 5	11 x 12
		12 − 8	16 − 8	5 x 6	12 x 12
		12 − 7	16 − 7	5 x 7	
		12 − 6	17 − 9	5 x 8	
		12 − 5	17 − 8	5 x 9	
		12 − 4	18 − 9	5 x 12	
		12 − 3			

Facts of the Week

<u>Week #1</u>: 8 + 2; 7 + 3; 6 + 4; 9 + 2; 9 + 3; 9 + 4; 9 + 5; 9 + 6; 9 + 7; 9 + 8

<u>Week #2</u>: 5 + 5; 6 + 6; 7 + 7; 8 + 8; 9 + 9

<u>Week #3</u>: 10 − 8; 10 − 7; 10 − 6; 3 x 3; 3 x 4

<u>Week #4</u>: 8 + 3; 7 + 4; 6 + 5; 10 − 5; 3 x 8

<u>Week #5</u>: 8 + 4; 7 + 5; 10 − 4; 10 − 3; 10 − 2

<u>Week #6</u>: 8 + 5; 7 + 6; 11 − 9; 12 − 9; 13 − 9

<u>Week #7</u>: 8 + 6; 8 + 7; 14 − 9; 15 − 9; 3 x 7

<u>Week #8</u>: 16 − 9; 17 − 9; 18 − 9; 3 x 9; 4 x 5

<u>Week #9</u>: 11 − 8; 13 − 8; 3 x 6; 4 x 4; 5 x 5

<u>Week #10</u>: 11 − 4; 12 − 8; 13 − 4; 3 x 5; 5 x 6

<u>Week #11</u>: 11 − 7; 12 − 5; 16 − 7; 3 x 12; 5 x 8

<u>Week #12</u>: 12 − 3; 13 − 7; 14 − 7; 4 x 7; 5 x 7

<u>Week #13</u>: 11 − 5; 13 − 5; 17 − 8; 4 x 9; 5 x 12

<u>Week #14</u>: 12 − 4; 14 − 6; 15 − 6; 4 x 8; 5 x 9

<u>Week #15</u>: 11 − 6; 13 − 6; 14 − 5; 7 x 8; 4 x 6

<u>Week #16</u>: 11 − 2; 12 − 6; 15 − 7; 6 x 9; 6 x 12

<u>Week #17</u>: 11 − 3; 14 − 8; 15 − 8; 6 x 7; 6 x 6

<u>Week #18</u>: 12 − 7; 16 − 8; 6 x 8; 7 x 7; 7 x 9

<u>Week #19</u>: 4 x 12; 8 x 8; 8 x 9; 11 x 11; 9 x 9

<u>Week #20</u>: 8 x 12; 9 x 12; 7 x 12; 11 x 12; 12 x 12

–Fourth Grade Math–

Overview of Child Development in Fourth Grade

The gates of paradise have closed; the child has arrived on the earth. Steiner referred to this age (fourth and fifth grade) as the "heart of childhood". In fourth grade, the children start to find their way in the world. Their interactions with peers and adults can be challenging. They want to know more about the world, about personalities, and about good and evil. The stories of Norse mythology are of a great help with this, and the children are eager to learn all about it.

Local geography helps the students to orientate themselves in space. The students are introduced to grammar, singing in rounds, and musical notation. And in math, one of the most difficult concepts is introduced – fractions. The beautiful world of ONE falls to pieces, while they discover that there exists a new world of numbers in between any two whole numbers.

Curriculum Summary for Fourth Grade Math

The world of numbers
- GCF. *Greatest common factors* should be introduced and practiced.
- LCM. *Least common multiples* should be introduced and practiced. This is needed as preparation for finding common denominators with fractions.

The arithmetic facts
- *Keeping it fresh.* If all went well in third grade, then the whole class should be quite solid with their arithmetic facts. In fourth grade, we simply need to keep it fresh. Our *fourth grade arithmetic facts review sheets* may only be needed two or three times per week (depending upon the class). Oral mental arithmetic also helps to keep the arithmetic facts fresh. (See *All about the Fourth Grade Arithmetic Facts Practice Sheets* under *More Ideas for Teaching Third Grade Math* and *A Step-by-Step Progression for the Arithmetic Facts* found in the appendix.)
- *Challenging multiplication facts.* The teacher can select some challenging multiplication facts from the 13's through the 25's tables. Some of these can be done by the whole class, and some can be given just to those students needing an extra challenge. This work can be continued into fifth and sixth grade.

The four processes
- *Horizontal addition and subtraction.* It is still good for the students to practice strategies (perhaps learned in earlier grades) for addition and subtraction with numbers up to 1000. They should become fluent working problems like: $125 + 126$, $895 + 112$, $974 - 875$. This can either be done through written practice sheets or with oral mental arithmetic.
- *Vertical addition and subtraction.* This was introduced in third grade, but now, in fourth grade, we work with larger numbers. Regular practice is needed.
- *Vertical multiplication.* In third grade, we worked with single-digit multipliers. Now we can practice with two-digit and three-digit multipliers. Regular practice (but not too much!) is needed.
- *Vertical division* (long division). Fourth grade is the time to introduce vertical division (unless it was briefly introduced in third grade). Through the year, we can build up to four-step problems, but keep the divisors between 2 and 12 (e.g., $15288 \div 6$). Regular practice (but not too much!) is needed.

Measurement. We should review third grade measurement, and begin doing simple conversion problems.

Fractions
- The goal in fourth grade is for the children to develop a sense for fractions – to bring them to an understanding of what a fraction is. *Too much of an emphasis on procedural skills with fractions will likely overwhelm many of the students, make it harder for them to develop a sense for fractions, and leave them hating fractions.*
- *By the end of fourth grade*, the students should have a basic understanding of fractions, including problems similar to those found in the following list. Again, *keep it simple!*
  - Give two other fractions that are equivalent to two-thirds.
  - What is one-fifth of 35? What is $\frac{2}{3}$ of 12?

Fourth Grade Math

- Mr. Jones has twenty students in his class. If one-quarter of the class is outside, then how many students are outside?
- How can two apples be divided fairly between four people? Between six people?
- The students should become at ease with fraction problems like these:

$\frac{3}{5} + \frac{1}{5} = \underline{}$ $\qquad$ $1\frac{1}{6} + \frac{4}{6} = \underline{}$ $\qquad$ $\frac{3}{4} - \frac{1}{3} = \underline{}$ $\qquad$ $\frac{3}{5} \times \frac{1}{2} = \underline{}$ $\qquad$ $5 \div \frac{1}{4} = \underline{}$

$\frac{5}{6} + \frac{1}{2} = \underline{}$ $\qquad$ $\frac{7}{12} - \frac{3}{12} = \underline{}$ $\qquad$ $1\frac{5}{8} - \frac{6}{8} = \underline{}$ $\qquad$ $\frac{2}{3} \times 12 = \underline{}$ $\qquad$ $\frac{1}{4} \div \frac{1}{12} = \underline{}$

- *Types of fractions.* Although proper (i.e., "normal") fractions receive the most attention, improper fractions and mixed numbers should also be introduced.
- *Equivalent fractions.* The students should clearly understand the idea of equivalent fractions (e.g., that ¾ is the same as ⁶/₈).
- *Common denominators* are introduced, and by the end of the year, the students should be at ease with them.
- With fractions, we work from the whole to the parts, and from the parts to the whole.
- *All four processes* with (simple, proper) fractions should be introduced.

Recommended Reading for Fourth Grade Math

- Henning Anderson, *Active Arithmetic*. AWSNA Publications.
- Herman von Baravalle, *The Teaching Of Arithmetic And The Waldorf School Plan*. Waldorf School Monographs, 1967, third edition.
- Dorothy Harrer, *Math Lessons For Elementary Grades*. AWSNA Publications.
- Christoph Jaffke, *Rhythms, Rhymes, Games and Songs for the Lower School*. Published by the Pedagogische Forschung Stelle, Der Bund der Freien Waldorf Schule in Stuttgart.
- Ron Jarman, *Teaching Mathematics in Rudolf Steiner Schools for Classes I-VIII*, Hawthorn press, Gloucestershire, 1998. (We recommend this book for ideas for fourth grade and up.)
- Lipping Ma, *Knowing and Teaching Elementary Mathematics*. Lawrence Erlbaum Assoc. Publishers 1919, London.
- Ernst Schuberth, *Teaching Mathematics for First and Second Grades in Waldorf Schools*. Rudolf Steiner College Press. (Especially the section about math weaknesses, pages 59 and up.)
- John A. van de Walle, *Elementary and Middle School Mathematics*. Virginia Commonwealth University, Longman, NY.

Lessons and Topics for Fourth Grade Math

Scheduling

The curriculum calls again for twelve weeks of math (three main lesson blocks of four weeks each), with one week of review at the end of the school year.

Don't forget!!

- *Every day*, we should review the previous day's lesson.
- *Every day*, we should bring something new to the children.
- *Every day*, the students should practice the new material and selected review topics.

Practice and review (of old material)

- During each math main lesson, we should be sure to practice the material from previous blocks and previous grades *for at least a half hour every day.*

Fourth Grade Math

- Most of the topics listed below were introduced some time ago. In order for the children to learn a topic well, it needs to be systematically reviewed. Obviously, all previous topics cannot be reviewed every day. The teacher needs to decide which topics are the most important to review each day. Some of these topics may need to be reviewed and practiced nearly every day, whether the class is in a math block, or not. As a general guideline, the class should practice 30 minutes daily, when in a math block, and about 10 minutes daily (in the morning) when not in a math block. (Also see *Review and Practice* under *Principles of Waldorf Education* above.)

Regarding fourth grade fractions
- *Caution!!* Often in Waldorf circles, you hear it said regarding the math curriculum, that "fourth grade is fractions". It is true that the introduction to fractions is an important part of the fourth grade year. However, in terms of classroom time spent in math lessons, work with fractions should not dominate everything else. Review and practice of concepts introduced in third grade, such as measurement and vertical arithmetic, is very important, as well as continued practice with horizontal arithmetic.
- *Keep it simple!* Everything listed here (for fourth grade) is intended as part of an introduction to fractions. There will be much more work with fractions in the coming years.
- It is not yet the goal to develop mastery of fraction skills – much of this is done in fifth and sixth grade. *Too much of an emphasis on procedural skills with fractions will likely overwhelm many of the students, make it harder for them to develop a sense for fractions, and leave them hating fractions.*
- The goal in fourth grade is for the children to develop a sense for fractions – to bring them to an understanding of what a fraction is. This is the foundation for studying fractions in future years.

The world of numbers
- *Greatest common factor* (GCF).
    - For example, we can ask, "What is the GCF of 30 and 24?" They then make one list of the factors of 24 (which is 1, 2, 3, 4, 6, 8, 12, 24), and another list of the factors of 30 (which is 1, 2, 3, 5, 6, 10, 15, 30). We can then see that the common factors are: 1, 2, 3, 6, and that 6 is the GCF.
    - After some practice, they should be able to do simple GCF problems in their heads.
- *Least common multiple* (LCM).
    - For example, we can ask, "What is the LCM of 4 and 6?" They then make a list of the multiples of 4 (i.e., numbers that are in the 4's table), and another list of the multiples of 6. They can then see that 12 is the LCM.
    - After some practice, they should be able to do simple LCM problems in their heads.
    - A good amount of LCM practice should happen before the second fraction main lesson when finding *least common denominators* is important.
- Number dictations should still happen occasionally in fourth grade. The children should be fluent with writing and reading numbers well into the millions. We can include fractions in our number dictations.
- Place value can be briefly reviewed and practiced.

Arithmetic facts
- Even if all went well in third grade with the learning of the arithmetic facts, there is still much work to be done in fourth grade, so that the facts are not forgotten. They should be practiced briefly, nearly every day, either through oral mental arithmetic, or with written practice sheets. Our *Fourth Grade Arithmetic Facts Review Sheets* are available for free download at **www.JamieYorkPress.com**.
- *Division with remainders*. This was begun in third grade. For example, we can give 33÷6, and their answer should be "5 with a remainder of 3". We could also tell the students to take some number (e.g., 30) and divide it by 1, 2, 3, 4, etc. They can discover patterns with this.
- *Challenging multiplication facts*. The teacher can select some challenging multiplication facts from the 13's through the 25's tables. Some of these can be done by the whole class, and some can be given just to those students needing an extra challenge. This work can be continued into fifth and sixth grade.
- The arithmetic facts can now be practiced in a more challenging way. For example, we can toss a beanbag or a tennis ball to a student as we call out a number. The student then answers with a multiplication or division fact while he throws the ball back. For example, if the teacher says 28, then

Fourth Grade Math

the student could give a variety of answers, such as: 2x14, 14x2, 7x4, 28x1, or 56÷2, 112÷4 etc. After working with one number, the students can write down all the different possibilities for that number.

<u>Working horizontally.</u> We should practice strategies (perhaps learned in earlier grades) for addition and subtraction, with numbers up to 1000. The students should become fluent with problems like 125 + 126, 895 + 112, 974 – 875. This can either be done through written practice sheets or with oral mental arithmetic.

<u>Working vertically</u>
- *Everyday,* we should practice vertical addition, subtraction, multiplication and division. However, keep in mind, that some students will slowly, over time, gain mastery over vertical arithmetic. Be sure that these students don't become anxious about it; they should still be learning joyfully!
- *Vertical addition and subtraction.* This is continued from what was done in third grade, but now with larger numbers. Regular practice is needed.
- *Vertical multiplication.*
  - In third grade, we worked with single-digit multipliers. Starting in the second math block of fourth grade, we can practice with two-digit and three-digit multipliers. Regular practice is needed.
  - Be sure to read *A step-by-step progression for vertical multiplication* under *More Ideas for Teaching Fourth Grade Math* below.
- *Vertical (long) division.*
  - Most likely, vertical division is new to the fourth grade class. Over the course of the year, we can build up to four-step problems, but keep the divisors between 2 and 12 (e.g., 15288÷6). Two-digit divisors (e.g., 1909÷23) should wait until fifth grade.
  - It can be helpful to introduce vertical division with a story, but be careful that the stories are not too elaborate, and that the details are relevant to the mathematical concepts.
  - Vertical division doesn't have to be a blind procedure. The children can be shown, to some degree, why it works. **Be sure to read** *A step-by-step progression for long division* **under** *More Ideas for Teaching Fourth Grade Math* **below.**
  - *Teach that math is flexible!* Students should feel that there are different ways to solve a given math problem, even though showing multiple methods may not always be practical. In the case of vertical division, it is good to show different methods to the students. Parents, who are from different countries, can show the class how they learned to do division. The students don't need to understand these different methods, but they can appreciate that other methods exist.
  - When the children begin practicing vertical division, it is necessary to lead them step-by-step through the procedure.
  - The sequential steps in long division are as follows (using the two-step division example 152÷4):
    1. First, we ask: "How many times does 4 go into 15?" (Answer: 3)
    2. Multiply 3x4 and then write it under the 15.
    3. Subtract to get a remainder of 3.
    4. Bring down the next digit.
    5. Repeat the above process until the problem is finished.

  ```
        38
     ┌─────
   4 │ 152
       - 12
        ───
         32
       - 32
        ───
          0
  ```

  - We should try to be very consistent and formulate the same questions during the process each time we do a long division problem.[31]
  - Once again, be sure that the class doesn't get overwhelmed with too many vertical division problems that are too difficult. It will be practiced much more in fifth and sixth grade.
  - Check answers to division problems by multiplying (e.g., for 2292÷6 = 382, multiply 6 x 382 to make sure that it's equal to 2292).

---

[31] Herman von Baravalle, *The Teaching of Arithmetic and the Waldorf School Plan.*

Fourth Grade Math

Mental arithmetic
- Practice mental arithmetic daily (for 10 minutes or less), and continue to develop strategies.
- Work up to calculations like:
  $400 - 12$; $798 + 5$; 3×400; 28×100; $1000 - 25$; $3000 - 205$; $8000 - 2700$; 40×70; 300×5.
- *"Halfway" problems.* Simple variations of these problems may have been introduced in second grade and third grade, but now we can include more complicated variations, like:
  - What number is halfway between 14 and 32?
  - What number is halfway between 16 and 86?
  - What number is halfway between 250 and 350?
  - What number is halfway between 250 and 280?
  - What number is halfway between 600 and 1200?
  - What number is halfway between 600 and 1100?
  - What number is halfway between 25 and 30?
- In fourth grade, it can be helpful (and fun!) to ask the students to find as many strategies as possible. Here are a few possible strategies (using the example "What's halfway between 14 and 32?"):
  - *Estimate and check.* Estimate the answer, check it, and adjust until you finally get it. (This is probably what most students try to do at first.) With the given example ("What's halfway between 14 and 32?") a student might first estimate 22, but then checks his answer and finds that 22 is 8 away from 14, but 22 is 10 away from 32. So he moves his answer up by one to get 23.
  - Add half the difference to the smaller number (probably the most common real strategy). The difference between 32 and 14 is 18. The answer is then 9 more than 14, which is 23.
  - Cut each number in half, and add the results together. The answer is then 7+16, which is 23.
  - Start at each number and count toward the middle simultaneously.
  - Start at some easy number in between, and then determine the average of the differences from that number and the two given numbers. Using the above example, we could choose 20, so the differences would be 6 and 12. Then find the average of these differences (which would be 9) and add that to the smaller number: $14 + 9 = 23$.
  - Add the two numbers and divide by two, which is the standard average formula. $\frac{14+32}{2} = 23$.

Measurement. Review the material from the third grade measurement main lesson. We should practice conversion problems like: 50 feet = __ yards; 26 inches = __ feet; 5 gallons = __ cups, etc.

Word Problems
- Simple written word problems are now introduced. Here are some examples of word problems to be done in fourth grade:
  - How can we divide $2292 evenly between six people?
    (This problem can be worked on in groups as part of an introduction to the full process for vertical division. See *A Step-by-Step Progression for Vertical (Long) Division* below.)
  - If we cut 8 apples into quarters, how many pieces do we have?
  - If Mary's mother buys oranges for $4.50 and peaches for $3.10, how much does she have to pay? If she gives the cashier a $10 bill, what should she get back for change? (Give many problems like this where the students need to determine how much change is given.)
- *Our puzzle and game book.* Fourth grade can also be a great time to bring riddles and puzzle problems to the class. Our *Making Math Meaningful Puzzle and Game Book* is intended as a resource for math teachers in grades four through twelve, in part to supplement the normal classroom material. It provides ideas for that "something different".

Fourth Grade Math

Math Main Lesson Block #1: An Introduction to Fractions

<u>New material and content</u>
- In this block, the students discover a new number world.
- Language is an important part of understanding fractions. They become familiar with new words like numerator, denominator, mixed number, improper fraction, etc.
- Our goal is to bring the students to a basic understanding of what a fraction is (e.g., what $^5/_8$ really means).
- *Equivalent fractions.* The students should clearly understand the idea of equivalent fractions (e.g., that ¾ is the same as $^6/_8$).
- The students work primarily with proper fractions, but also become familiar with improper fractions and mixed numbers.
- *Don't forget to review and practice!* Previously introduced material needs to be reviewed, practiced, and furthered. (See above *Practice and review of old material* under *Lessons and Topics for Fourth Grade Math*.)

<u>Movement</u>
- *The first week.*
  - *Day #1.*
  On the first day, we introduce fractions with food (that will be eaten!) that is divided into pieces. We say clearly that you divide it first in half, then half again, and so on. That's it for the first day!
  - *Day #2.*
  On the second day of the block, we can "move" the fraction from the first day. For example, if we divided a cake into 12 pieces on the first day, then we can "walk it" on the second day. Every step represents a piece of the cake. The class then walks and speaks the fraction:

  $$\frac{1}{12}, \frac{2}{12}, \frac{3}{12}, \ldots \ldots \text{ up to } \frac{11}{12}, \text{ and } \frac{12}{12} \text{ (but we say "one")}$$

  And then we do the whole thing backwards! While doing this, we make the students aware of how to properly pronounce the fractions. After this has been worked on, we can then do a new example of dividing something into pieces (e.g., dividing four apples into six pieces).
  - *Day #3.*
  If we divided four apples into six pieces on the previous day, we can now walk by sixths until we reach 4.

  $$\frac{1}{6}, \frac{2}{6}, \frac{3}{6}, \frac{4}{6}, \frac{5}{6}, \text{ "One",}$$
  $$1\frac{1}{6}, 1\frac{2}{6}, 1\frac{3}{6}, 1\frac{4}{6}, 1\frac{5}{6}, \text{ "Two",}$$
  $$2\frac{1}{6}, 2\frac{2}{6}, 2\frac{3}{6}, 2\frac{4}{6}, 2\frac{5}{6}, \text{ "Three",}$$
  $$3\frac{1}{6}, 3\frac{2}{6}, 3\frac{3}{6}, 3\frac{4}{6}, 3\frac{5}{6}, \text{ "Four!".}$$

  And then we do it backwards!
  After this has been worked on, we can then do another new example of dividing something into pieces.
  - *Day #4 and #5.*
  We build very systematically on what we have done in the first three days.

Fourth Grade Math

- *During the second week*, we give the class a fraction and they walk forward (or backwards) to a certain number.

  <u>Example</u>: We tell the class to start at $3\frac{3}{4}$ and step up to 6. Their steps are then:

  $$3\frac{3}{4},\ 4,\ 4\frac{1}{4},\ 4\frac{2}{4},\ 4\frac{3}{4},\ 5,\ 5\frac{1}{4},\ 5\frac{2}{4},\ 5\frac{3}{4},\ 6.$$

  <u>Example</u>: We tell the class to start at $3\frac{6}{8}$ and step up to 6. Their steps are then:

  $$3\frac{6}{8},\ 3\frac{7}{8},\ 4,\ 4\frac{1}{8},\ 4\frac{2}{8},\ 4\frac{3}{8},\ 4\frac{4}{8},\ 4\frac{5}{8},\ 4\frac{6}{8},\ 4\frac{7}{8},\ 5,\ 5\frac{1}{8},\ 5\frac{2}{8},\ 5\frac{3}{8},\ 5\frac{4}{8},\ 5\frac{5}{8},\ 5\frac{6}{8},\ 5\frac{7}{8},\ 6.$$

  <u>Example</u>: We tell the class to start at $1\frac{2}{6}$ and step down to zero. Their steps are then:

  $$1\frac{2}{6},\ 1\frac{1}{6},\ 1,\ \frac{5}{6},\ \frac{4}{6},\ \frac{3}{6},\ \frac{2}{6},\ \frac{1}{6},\ 0.$$

- The students should become more at ease with the fraction line; it becomes part of them.
- The students should write down what they have practiced into their practice books (e.g., they should write the same row of fraction steps from memory on the same day that they did it).

<u>Working with manipulatives</u>

- *Fractions with food.* For the first week, we suggest starting the block with various edible objects (e.g., pies, pizza, pancakes, apples, chocolate) – preferably, each day, something of a different shape than the day before. For example, one day we work with pizza (circle), the next day apples (sphere), the next day a slice of bread (rectangle), the next day string cheese (line), and on the last day, a tall, round cake (which can be cut in many different ways).
- *Fractions with paper.* It is best for the children to create their own manipulatives for fractions. After we have tasted our fractions, we can then cut fractions from various shapes on paper: circles, triangles, rectangles, and squares. Again, the students need to experience different shapes for the same fraction. These paper fractions should be glued into their main lesson books.
- *Fraction envelopes.* The children should also make extra sets of these paper fractions and keep them in an envelope. These "fraction envelopes" will be used later to help with adding, subtracting, and finding equivalent fractions.

<u>Bookwork</u>

- The students should draw some of the "food fractions" that were done in class.
- They should include several examples with "paper fractions" (the fractions should be written on the shapes).
- One page should have different cuttings for each fraction.
- The main lesson book should also include the key concepts, such as: numerator, denominator, mixed number, improper fraction, etc.
- Be sure to visit our website (**www.JamieYorkPress.com**) to see full-color pages from students' main lesson books.

Fourth Grade Math

Math Main Lesson Block #2: Addition and Subtraction of Fractions

New material and content
- *Finding common denominators.*
  - This concept needs a good deal of practice!
  - It is best for the children to have had a fair amount of practice with *Least Common Multiples* (LCM) before the start of this main lesson block.
    Example: What is the common denominator for $5/6$ and $1/4$?
    This is the same as asking: "Where do the denominators meet?" The students should then make a table, similar to this:

6	4
6	4
12	8
	12

  - These problems can be made visual by using the cutout pieces from their "fraction envelopes" (see *Math Main Lesson Block #1*).
  - For more visual ideas, see John E. van de Walle's book, *Elementary and middle school mathematics*.
- *Adding and subtraction with unlike denominators.* Once the students understand how to find common denominators between two fractions with unlike denominators, we can introduce adding and subtracting such fractions. Limit this to fairly simple proper fractions (but the answers may exceed 1).

  Example: $\frac{5}{6} + \frac{1}{2}$

  Solution: To do this, the students should work with the pieces in their fraction envelope. They take 5 pieces of $1/6$ and 1 piece of $1/2$ and see how they fit together. They should discover that $1/2 = 3/6$. Therefore, $5/6 + 1/2$ is the same as $5/6 + 3/6$. The students can now easily see that together they make $8/6$, which can also be written as $1\frac{2}{6}$ or $1\frac{1}{3}$.

  Example: $\frac{3}{4} - \frac{1}{3}$

  Solution: This could be the most difficult problem they do in this main lesson block. They should again use the pieces from their fraction envelope, as with the previous example. In this case, they would be working with 12 as the common denominator.

- *Vertical multiplication.*
  - In third grade, we worked with single-digit multipliers. Now we can introduce two-digit and three-digit multipliers.
  - Be sure to read *A step-by-step progression for vertical multiplication* under *More Ideas for Teaching Fourth Grade Math* below.
- *Don't forget to review and practice!* Previously introduced material needs to be reviewed, practiced, and furthered. (See above *Practice and review of old material* under *Lessons and Topics for Fourth Grade Math*.)

Movement
- In the first block, the class "walked" fractions. Now we can walk different fractions at the same time.
  Example: (Using $1/8$, $1/4$, $1/2$) The students line up next to each other. The $1/8$ students take a small step for every count, while the $1/4$ students take a medium step (twice the size of the $1/8$ students) with every other count, and the $1/2$ students step (four times the size of the $1/8$ students) with every four counts, starting at four-eighths. And they continue to move along in his manner.

Working with manipulatives. The students can use their fraction envelopes when necessary.

Bookwork
- The new concepts of this block (adding and subtracting fractions with unlike denominators, and vertical multiplication with two and three-digit multipliers) need to be thoroughly explained in the main lesson books. They should show the step-by-step processes. Use space, color, and drawings. Be creative!
- Be sure to visit our website (**www.JamieYorkPress.com**) to see full-color pages from students' main lesson books.

Fourth Grade Math

Math Main Lesson Block #3: Multiplication and Division of Fractions

<u>New material and content</u>
- *Multiplication with fractions.*
  - The typical approach for multiplying fractions is to simply multiply the numerators and multiply the denominators. However, without any buildup or explanation, this becomes a *blind trick*. Instead, we should lead the students to discover this for themselves. It thus becomes a *strategic trick*.
  - In order for the students to truly understand fraction multiplication, we need to translate the mathematical concepts into spoken language. We should, of course, start with simple examples, such as: ½ x ½ = ¼ which means, "one half of one half equals one fourth."
  - We should slowly build up to more complicated problems like: $\frac{2}{3} \times \frac{2}{5} = \frac{4}{15}$
  - We need to find ways to make it visible – perhaps in a different way each day. (Visit our website **www.JamieYorkPress.com** to see full-color drawings of this.)
  - After several days of translating and drawing, the students slowly come to understand the *strategic trick* for multiplying fractions: we have to multiply the two numerators together and multiply the two denominators together.
- *Division with fractions.*
  - Our goal, once again, is to lead the students to discovering the *strategic trick* for themselves.
  - As with fraction multiplication, we should introduce fraction division by translating the mathematical concepts into spoken language.
  - Here is a step-by-step progression:

12÷6= 2	How many times does 6 fit into 12?
12÷4= 3	How many times does 4 fit into 12?
12÷3 = 4	How many times does 3 fit into 12?
12÷2= 6	How many times does 2 fit into 12?
12÷1= 12	How many times does 1 fit into 12?
12÷½ = 24	How many times does ½ fit into 12?
12÷⅓ = 36	How many times does ⅓ fit into 12?
½÷¼ = 2	How many times does ¼ fit into ½?

  - In this way, the students should discover for themselves that the *strategic trick* is to multiply by the reciprocal of the second fraction. Even if this discovery is led by a few of the "quicker" students in the class, it is valuable for the whole class to see that it comes from some process.
- *Don't forget to review and practice!* Previously introduced material needs to be reviewed, practiced, and furthered. (See above *Practice and review of old material* under *Lessons and Topics for Fourth Grade Math*.)

<u>Movement</u>. The movement exercises for fractions slowly transform from the physical to lively imaginative thinking. Starting now, the students have to do the math movement internally, instead of doing it physically. This progresses, until in middle school, it has become a lively, inner movement.

<u>Working with manipulatives</u>. The students can either cut and paste fractions, or draw them.

<u>Bookwork</u>
- The students should draw the new concepts of fraction multiplication and fraction division into their main lesson books.
- Be sure to visit our website (**www.JamieYorkPress.com**) to see full-color pages from students' main lesson books.

Fourth Grade Math

More Ideas for Teaching Fourth Grade Math
(Be sure to reread the section, *Thoughts on Teaching Math in the Lower Grades*, found at the start of this book.)

All about the fourth grade arithmetic facts *review* sheets, and daily practice

- Free download!! You can download our fourth grade arithmetic facts review sheets *for free* from our website: **www.JamieYorkPress.com**.
- This is review! These math fact sheets are intended as review of the *Third Grade Arithmetic Facts Practice Sheets*. It is important that the students first do those third grade *Practice Sheets* (and are very familiar with the 105 facts in them) before doing these fourth grade *Review Sheets*.
- Timing. Each sheet has 30 problems. There are 100 sheets in the whole set. A class should do three sheets per week (on average) throughout the fourth grade year.
- Caution! This should be fun and easy for the students. If successful, this builds their confidence. It is important to make sure that these sheets don't become torture for the students. Try to de-emphasize the importance of speed (this can wait until fifth grade). Help the students realize that improvement is important.
- A special note regarding division with remainders. Towards the end of the *Third Grade Arithmetic Facts Practice Sheets*, we introduced division with remainders. On those sheets, these remainder problems looked something like $31 \div 5 = \_\_ r \_\_$, which warned the students that they were remainder problems. In contrast, the *Fourth Grade Review Sheets* (found here) don't warn the students of the remainder problems. Therefore, the problem is simply given as $31 \div 5 = \_\_$, and the student should write the answer as 6 r 1. The students should know that on every sheet (of 30 problems) there is always one remainder problem. This makes it consistent, and perhaps fun for the students to find the mystery remainder problem.
- What comes next? The next set of practice sheets is titled *Fifth Grade Arithmetic Facts Speed Sheets*. They are designed to increase the calculation speed of the students.
- The whole picture. The 30 problems listed on a particular sheet are only a part of a day's math practice, which should only take about five minutes of class time. **It would be very unfortunate if daily math practice consisted of nothing more than the 30 arithmetic facts practice problems that appear on these sheets.**
- The elements of math practice. The following list shows some of the aspects to consider when planning math practice for the day.
    - *Arithmetic facts review sheet*. The teacher copies by hand the 30 problems from a given day (i.e., these fourth grade arithmetic facts review sheets) onto paper to be photocopied.[32] (about 5 minutes)
    - *Mental arithmetic*. The teacher may decide to read the first 6 problems out loud.
    - *Extra math practice problems*. There should be a few problems that the teacher comes up with and writes on the board. The students copy them into their practice books and work out the answers. These problems also include practice and review of material covered in previous math blocks. (This takes 20-25 minutes if the class is in a math block, otherwise only 5 minutes.)
    - *Challenge problems*. It is important that the last few problems (that the teacher adds on) be more challenging in order to keep the "quicker" students fully engaged.
- And what happens if…? We hope that it won't happen, but even when most of the class is doing well with these sheets, there may be a few children who still haven't solidly learned their arithmetic facts. In order to help these children, it may be helpful to give them a multiplication/division table (i.e., a square for the tables). Additionally, these students could study the basic arithmetic problems with flashcards during morning practice time.

---

[32] *Saving paper*. Try to find ways to reduce the amount of paper being used. For example, rather than using one sheet of paper each day, each side could be divided into three columns (i.e., 6 days per sheet). This is one of many ways to help develop an environmental consciousness in the students.

Fourth Grade Math

A step-by-step progression for vertical multiplication (with two-digit multipliers)

Notes:
- The students should draw columns for the place values: thousands, hundreds, tens, and ones. It may be that graphing paper (with square grids) is helpful for students.
- We strongly recommend that students write a "0" (in all grades) instead of a blank for the placeholder. This better shows that we are actually multiplying with tens, hundreds, thousands, etc.
- We recommend that, in the end, the students avoid writing the small "carry" number on top of the multiplication problem. Instead, they should simply keep it in their heads.

Step #1:

```
                  4 7   →   40+7
              x   3 6   →   30+6
                 ─────
  6x7  =          4 2
  6x40 =          2 4 0
  30x7 =          2 1 0
  30x40=      + 1 2 0 0
              ─────────
                1 6 9 2
```

Step #2:

```
                  ² ⁴
                  4 7
              x   3 6
                 ─────
  47x6  =         2 8 2
  47x30 =     + 1 4 1 0
              ─────────
                1 6 9 2
```

Step #3:

```
          ² ⁴
          4 7
      x   3 6
         ─────
          2 8 2
      + 1 4 1 0
      ─────────
        1 6 9 2
```

Step #4: (Without the carry digits!)

```
          4 7
      x   3 6
         ─────
          2 8 2
      + 1 4 1 0
      ─────────
        1 6 9 2
```

Fourth Grade Math

A Step-by-Step Progression for Vertical (Long) Division
(How to build up to an understanding of vertical division)

Note:
- The below sequence of steps works with the three-step division problem 2292÷6, which is likely too difficult of a starting point for the children. It would be better to start with a two-step problem, such as 152÷4.
- This is only intended to give the teacher a sense of how to introduce vertical division in a way that builds up to an understanding of where the final procedure comes from.

Step #1: (As a Story Problem):
The whole class could use play money in small groups, and, in a practical manner, do what is shown here. This could be done with different numbers each day, for several days, before moving to the next stage. Nothing should be written down yet.

The gist of the story might look something like this:

Sally needs to divide $2292 evenly between 6 people. At first, she gives $200 to each person. This means she just gave away $1200 dollars, so she has (2292–1200) $1092 left. She then gives $150 more to each person, resulting in giving away (6x150) $900, and leaving her now with (1092–900) $192. Then she gives $20 to each person, which leaves her with (192–120) $72 dollars. Lastly, she gives away $12 to each person, which leaves her with nothing. Each person ends up with (200+150+20+12) $382. Therefore, we can say that 2292÷6 = 382.

Step #2: (Accounting Format):
The actions of the above problem can be written like this:

Pot of Money		**Each Person**
2292		
− 1200	← x6 ←	200
1092		
− 900	← x6 ←	150
192		
− 120	← x6 ←	20
72		
− 72	← x6 ←	+ 12
0		Total = 382

Step #3: (Flexible Vertical Division):
This method looks similar to normal vertical division, but is flexible. Students can do it in many different ways to get the correct answer, as opposed to normal vertical division, which is rigid (e.g., the first digit must be a "3", etc.).

Flexible Vertical Division looks like this:

```
       200+150+20+12 = 382
    6 ⟌ 2292
       −1200
        1092
       − 900
         192
        − 120
           72
         − 72
            0
```

Step #4: (Vertical Division with Zeroes):
Now we can challenge the students to "give away the money" in a way such that you have to give away the correct number of hundreds first, then the correct number of tens, and finally the correct number of ones.

It looks like this:

```
       300+80+2 = 382
    6 ⟌ 2292
       −1800
         492
        − 480
           12
         − 12
            0
```

Step #5: ("Normal" Vertical Division):
This is the usual way that vertical division is done in this country. If the whole build up is done successfully, then students may be really excited about learning this as a shortcut for what they already have learned.

```
           382
    6 ⟌ 2292
        − 18
          49
        − 48
          12
        − 12
           0
```

–Fifth Grade Math–

Overview of Child Development in Fifth Grade

We leave the troubled lives of the Norse gods behind as the sun heralds a beautiful start of a new day. This is now the middle of the grade school years. In fifth grade, temperaments and talents become more visible, and the student communicates easily between the inner and the outer world. There is an increased interest in social interactions. Breathing and blood circulation become harmonized. The proportions of the physical body are in harmony, thereby allowing for graceful physical movements. The child's cognitive capacities are increasing, which is accompanied by a desire to be challenged. The students want to improve their work because they want to be proud of their work. They want and need constructive feedback.

The fifth grade history curriculum, which starts with the ancient cultures and culminates in Greek history, develops their orientation in time. In language arts, the students are introduced to the verb tenses. In music, the class can now learn to sing multi-part harmonies.

The students have matured and now have an ability for a deeper understanding of more complex, mathematical concepts. This is the time to become confident in math concepts from previous years (e.g., vertical division, multiplication, fractions, etc.). We give the students more challenging problems, which slowly, with regular practice, help to increase their skill level. It is in fifth (and sixth) grade that the students solidify their foundation in basic arithmetic. The new topic of decimal fractions sets the stage for the introduction to percents in sixth grade.

Curriculum Summary for Fifth Grade Math

Fractions
- The students should become fluent when working with common and unlike denominators.
- All four processes (+, –, x, ÷) with common fractions and mixed numbers should be practiced regularly.

Decimal fractions. The number world of decimal fractions is introduced. Place value practice supports this.

Measurement
- The metric system is introduced, which can be nicely integrated with decimal fractions.
- Distance, weight, and capacity (volume) of the metric system should all be introduced.
- Review of the U.S. measurement system should be integrated into our work with the metric system.

Geometry
- *Freehand geometry*. The students should create many beautiful drawings of circles, squares, triangles, angles, divisions of the circle, etc., all freehand, without the aid of a ruler or compass. The accuracy required with this takes great focus and will.
- We can bring an imaginative picture of the *Pythagorean Theorem* at this time.
- We can also introduce *perimeter and area*.

The Wonder of Number. This can be a central theme for a creative main lesson. The idea is to bring several properties of numbers that will leave the students with a feeling of wonder. There are many topics and mathematical properties that can accomplish this (e.g., *Square and Triangular Numbers, Powers of Two, Divisibility Rules, Perfect Numbers, Sum and Difference Theorems*, etc.). (See details under *Math Main Lesson Block #3: Geometry and the Wonder of Number* below.)

Review and Practice
- Consolidation of skills (that were introduced in earlier years) is a major theme for both fifth grade and sixth grade math. Systematic review and practice is needed throughout the year.
- It is especially important to review (and further) all work with vertical arithmetic (addition, subtraction, long multiplication, and long division), and all work with fractions.

Arithmetic facts
- Review and practice of the arithmetic facts is still important. This can be done as part of daily oral mental arithmetic, and further reinforced a few times per week with arithmetic fact practice sheets (e.g., our *fifth grade arithmetic facts speed sheets*).
- Also, work with challenging multiplication facts (e.g., selected from 13-25 tables) can be done, which may have been started in fourth grade.

Fifth Grade Math

Recommended Reading for Fifth Grade Math

- Henning Anderson, *Active Arithmetic*. AWSNA Publications.
- Herman von Baravalle, *The Teaching Of Arithmetic And The Waldorf School Plan*. Waldorf School Monographs, 1967, third edition.
- Julia E. Diggins, *String, Straight Edge & Shadow*. Jamie York Press.
- Dorothy Harrer, *Math Lessons For Elementary Grades*. AWSNA Publications.
- Christoph Jaffke, *Rhythms, Rhymes, Games and Songs for the Lower School*. Published by the Pedagogische Forschung Stelle, Der Bund der Freien Waldorf Schule in Stuttgart.
- Lipping Ma, *Knowing and Teaching Elementary Mathematics*. Lawrence Erlbaum Assoc. Publishers 1919, London.
- Ernst Schuberth, *Geometry Lessons in the Waldorf School, Volume 2*. AWSNA Publications. (Note: This is an excellent book, but, for the most part, what he has listed for fourth grade, we would recommend for fifth grade, and what he has listed for fifth grade, such as work with a compass and straight edge, we would recommend for sixth grade.)
- John A. van de Walle, *Elementary and Middle School Mathematics*. Virginia Commonwealth University, Longman, NY.
- Ron Jarman, *Teaching Mathematics in Rudolf Steiner Schools for Classes I-VIII*, Hawthorn press, Gloucestershire, 1998. (We recommend this book for ideas for fourth grade and up.)
- Malba Tahan, *The Man Who Counted,* W.W. Norton and Company, New York, 1993.

Lessons and Topics for Fifth Grade Math

Scheduling
> The curriculum calls again for twelve weeks of math (three main lesson blocks of four weeks each), with one week of review at the end of the school year.

Don't forget!!

- *Every day*, we should review the previous day's lesson.
- *Every day*, we should bring something new to the children.
- *Every day*, the students should practice the new material and selected review topics.

Practice and review (of old material)

- *Consolidation of skills (that were introduced in earlier years) is a major theme for both fifth grade and sixth grade math. Systematic review and practice is needed throughout the year.*
- Rudolf Steiner recommended one practice hour (skills class) per week for math beginning in fifth grade.
- During each math main lesson, we should be sure to practice the material from previous blocks and previous grades *for at least a half hour every day.*
- Most of the topics listed below were introduced some time ago. In order for the children to learn a topic well, it needs to be systematically reviewed. Obviously, all previous topics cannot be reviewed every day. The teacher needs to decide which topics are the most important to review each day. Some of these topics may need to be reviewed and practiced nearly every day, whether the class is in a math block, or not. As a general guideline, the class should practice 30 minutes daily, when in a math block, and about 10 minutes daily (in the morning) when not in a math block. (Also see *Review and Practice* under *Principles of Waldorf Education* above.)

Working vertically with the four processes. *Everyday* we should practice some problems using vertical addition, subtraction, multiplication, and division. We can also integrate work with decimals into this, as well as problems with extra zeroes at the end.
- *Vertical addition and subtraction.* Continued from what was done in fourth grade, but now with larger numbers. Regular practice is needed.

Fifth Grade Math

- *Vertical multiplication.* Simply continue and further what was done in fourth grade. Perhaps now we can even multiply two 4-digit numbers together. Regular practice is needed.
- *Vertical (long) division.* Last year, in fourth grade, vertical division was limited to single digit divisors. This year, we can work with two-digit divisors (e.g., 1909÷23), building up to problems like 63206÷65. Be sure to (at least occasionally) check answers to division problems by multiplying (e.g., with 1909÷23=83, we should multiply 83x23 to make sure that it's equal to 1909).

Fractions
- All four processes with the common fractions and mixed numbers need to be thoroughly practiced.
- Our work with fractions, which was begun last year, needs a good amount of attention. The students need to feel confident with fractions.
- *Addition and subtraction.* The students should become fluent in working with common denominators and at ease with unlike denominators.
- *Multiplying and dividing* common fractions should be thoroughly practiced.
- *Mixed numbers* should be worked with regularly, including all four processes.

Estimating. The students should learn to estimate before calculating a problem.

Arithmetic facts
- *Speed sheets.* Even if the class successfully learned all of their arithmetic facts in third and fourth grade, practicing these facts in fifth grade is still important. This can be done as part of daily oral mental arithmetic, and further reinforced a few times per week with arithmetic fact practice sheets. You can download our *fifth grade arithmetic facts speed sheets* for free from our website.
- *Challenging multiplication facts.* Previously, we had suggested that the fourth grade teacher could select some new multiplication facts from the 13's through the 25's tables. Some of these can be done by the whole class, and some can be given just to those students needing an extra challenge. This work may be continued in fifth (and sixth) grade.

Mental arithmetic
- Practice mental arithmetic daily (for 10 minutes or less).
- Work up to calculations like: 84 – 26; 423 – 60; 546 + 76; 40 x 600; 5.378 x 100; 24,000 ÷ 600.
- *"Halfway" problems.* We can continue doing problems that were done in earlier grades (e.g., "What is halfway between 26 and 56?"), but now we can add problems that work with fractions, like:
  - What number is halfway between $3/8$ and $7/8$?
  - What number is halfway between $3/7$ and $4/7$?
  - What number is halfway between 25.5 and 26.3?

Word Problems. Word problems given in fifth grade should be more practical, such as:
- If a pound of cheese is divided evenly between 8 people, then how much does each person get?
- 23 fifth graders are working on a garden project. Every one works 1½ hours. How many working-hours is that altogether?
- Simple *unit cost* problems, including:
  - If oranges cost 74¢ per pound, then how much do you need to pay for 5 pounds of oranges?
  - If 4 pounds of oranges cost $5.16, then what is the price per pound?
  - If 4 pounds of oranges cost $5.16, how much do 7 pounds of oranges cost?
  - If 4.3 pounds of oranges cost $5.16, then what is the price per pound?
  - If 4.3 pounds of oranges cost $5.16, then how much do 7 pounds of oranges cost?

Fifth Grade Math

<u>Puzzles</u>
- Fifth grade is a good time to give puzzles, but be careful to select a puzzle that is at the appropriate level. Puzzles that are too hard can be discouraging for many of the students. The right puzzle can bring joy into the classroom for all of the students.
- Our *Making Math Meaningful Puzzle and Game Book* is intended as a resource for math teachers in grades four through twelve, in part to supplement the normal classroom material. It provides ideas for that "something different".
- *Math Magic Trick.* Here is an example from our *Puzzle and Game Book*: Start with two numbers between 1 – 9. Add these two numbers together to get a third number. Add the second and third number together to get a fourth number. Add the third and fourth numbers together to get a fifth number. Continue this process until you have ten numbers. Add together all ten numbers. Divide by 11. This final answer will always be equal to the seventh number in your list.

Math Main Lesson Block #1: Decimal Fractions

<u>New material and content</u>
- *Decimal Fractions.*
  - We can begin with the question: what is the meaning of 'deca'? Some examples[33]: <u>deca</u>gon, <u>Dec</u>ember (the tenth month of the Roman calendar).
  - We should review our place value work in second and third grade. At that time, each step in place value (moving to the left) increased the value by a multiple of ten of that place. Now, with decimal fractions, each step taken to the right decreases the value of the place by a factor of ten.
  - *A fun exercise with decimals.*
    - There is a hat for each place value (e.g., thousands, hundreds, tens, ones, tenths, hundredths, thousandths). One student is the decimal point. Starting out simply, we could just work with three digits. So we line up three students and give each one a digit – for example, the left-most student gets a 7, the next student gets a 1, and the last student gets a 5.
    - The 'decimal' student then positions himself between two of the digits – assume for now between the 7 and the 1. Another student then takes the collection of hats, and gives the 'ones' hat to the student holding the 7, the 'tenths' hat to the student holding the 1, and the 'hundredths' hat to the student holding the 5. The class then reads it as "seven and fifteen hundredths".
    - We can then collect just the hats, and ask what happens if the decimal place moves one place to the left or right. The hats then get reassigned and the class reads the new number.
  - *Speech and language.*
    - In the second grade chapter of this book, we said that the teacher should be careful when saying numbers, so that an extra "and" isn't added in. For example, 270 should be spoken as "two-hundred-seventy", not "two-hundred-*and*-seventy".
    - Throughout fifth grade, we should always say "decimal fractions" instead of just "decimals". We should also speak these numbers in a way that shows they are fractions. For example, with 1.42, try to avoid saying "one point four two", but rather say, "one and forty-two hundredths". This may be phased out in sixth or seventh grade.

---

[33] Dorothy Harrer, *Math Lessons For Elementary Grades.*

- *Fluency and practice.* The students should quickly become comfortable with decimal fractions.
  - We can say to the students: "Make this number 10 times bigger, or 100 times smaller, etc."
  - The students need to be at ease when there are several digits behind the decimal point and be able to answer questions like: "What is bigger 1.78 or 1.76993?"
  - We should also practice rounding decimals.
  - We should show the students how most monetary systems are based on the decimal system.
  - We can bring digital time in relation to sporting events.
- The four processes with decimal fractions should also be introduced.
  - For vertical addition and subtraction of decimal fractions, place value is very important. Therefore, we need to make sure that we line up the decimal point.
  - We should also practice the four processes with decimal fractions orally (mental arithmetic) and in written horizontal form as well (e.g., $3.25x10 = \_\_$).
- *Simple equivalences.*
  - The students should discover that, for decimal fractions, we need to find equivalent fractions in tenths, hundredths, and thousandths. Examples are:
    - One half = ½ = 5/10 = 0.5;
    - 0.25 = 25/100 = ¼ , etc.
  - Practice of converting common fractions to decimal fractions is saved for the next math block.
- *Don't forget to review and practice – 30 minutes per day during a math main lesson!* Material that has been introduced in previous blocks and in previous years needs to be reviewed, practiced, and furthered. (See above *Practice and review of old material* under *Lessons and Topics for Fifth Grade Math.*)

Movement and manipulatives
- There are many exercises that the teacher can create. (See also "*A fun exercise with decimals*" above.)

Bookwork
- Be sure to visit our website (**www.JamieYorkPress.com**) to see full-color pages from students' main lesson books.

Math Main Lesson Block #2: The Metric System

New material and content
- This is the introduction to the metric system as a universal measurement language.
- The debate on whether the United States should adopt the metric system has been going on for nearly 200 years. The United States is one of the few countries in the world (Liberia and Burma being the others) that hasn't committed to adopting the metric system.
- In contrast to the U.S. measurement system, the metric system eliminates the need to deal with common fractions. The metric system is considered to be a simpler form of measurement. It is based on the decimal system (units of ten).
- Over the course of this main lesson block, the students should measure a great many objects using the metric system. Don't forget to estimate each time before you measure.
- In this block, we shall interweave the introduction of the metric system with a review and furthering of the U.S. system.
- We should *not* have the students practice converting given measurements from the U.S. system to the metric system (or vice versa). Instead, the students should experience measuring and estimating in both systems. Estimation is key!

Fifth Grade Math

- *Linear Measurement.*
  - In order to make it practical, we can begin, as we did in third grade, with measuring things in the classroom. We can measure students' heights, the perimeter of books, the lengths of desks, the blackboard, and the whole classroom. We can even measure the campus. We can use the students' rulers, or meter sticks, or tape measures. We should measure both in meters and in centimeters.
  - Always estimate before measuring!
  - From all of our measuring work, we can then introduce the other units of linear measurement: millimeter (mm), centimeter (cm), decimeter (dm), meter (m), decameter (dam), hectometer (hm), kilometer (km). The students need to get a sense that every step is a factor of ten.
  - The students should become comfortable with both the U.S. and the metric units.
  - *Simple conversions within the metric system.* The students should practice converting from one unit to the other (e.g., 7m = __ cm). Keep it simple. Much more of this should be practiced in the coming years.
- *Weight.*
  - The students should have many experiences with weighing objects, first in the U.S. system, and then in the metric system. Once again, it should be practical, and always remember to estimate before weighing.
  - Out of the practical work, the students should become comfortable with both the U.S. and the metric units.
    - U.S. system: ounces, pounds, tons.
    - Metric system: milligram (mg), centigram (cg), decigram (dg), gram (g), decagram (dag), hectogram (hg), kilogram (kg).
  - *Simple conversions within the metric system.* The students should practice converting from one unit to the other (e.g., 18kg = __ g).
- *Capacity (volume).*
  - Once again, the students should have many experiences weighing objects first in the U.S. system, and then in the metric system (e.g., fill up bottles, cans, tins, etc.). Again, it should be practical, and always remember to estimate before measuring.
  - The students should become comfortable with both the U.S. and the metric units.
    - U.S. system: teaspoon, tablespoon, fluid ounce, cup, pint, quart, and gallon.
    - Metric system: milliliter (mℓ), centiliter (cℓ), deciliter (dℓ), liter (ℓ), decaliter (daℓ), hectoliter (hℓ), kiloliter (kℓ)
- *Don't forget to review and practice – 30 minutes per day during a math main lesson!* Material that has been introduced in previous blocks and in previous years needs to be reviewed, practiced, and furthered. (See above *Practice and review of old material under Lessons and Topics for Fifth Grade Math.*)
  - *Reviewing and furthering decimals.* The material from the first block on decimal fractions needs to be reviewed and practiced. The students can now learn to convert from common fractions to decimal fractions, and vice versa.

Movement and manipulatives
- Through all of the hands-on work, there is much movement.
- Walking (or running!) various distances is also a good idea (e.g., have the whole class walk a distance of one kilometer away from the school).

Bookwork
- The students should make charts, tables, and graphs of measurements (estimations and actual). As always, the illustrations should be done beautifully.
- Be sure to visit our website (**www.JamieYorkPress.com**) to see full-color pages from students' main lesson books.

Fifth Grade Math

Math Main Lesson Block #3: Freehand Geometry and the Wonder of Number

<u>New material and content</u>
- *Timing and balance.* Given that there are two separate topics covered in this main lesson, it is important that we balance how much is done during any one day, and during the entire main lesson block. We recommend that an equal amount of time is spent on these three areas: geometry, wonder of number, and math practice/review.
- *Freehand geometry.*
  - Most of the drawings with this topic involve circles, rectangles, angles, and triangles, all with a good amount of variations.
    - After form drawing in the lower grades, we step right into freehand geometry in fifth grade. These geometrical drawings require extra care because they are so ordered. The drawings demand will forces from the students as they learn to follow the geometrical laws of the forms.
    - Freehand geometry also develops the feeling capacity for the ideal form itself. The connection with the archetypal forms has to come from the feeling level, and not yet out of the intellectual realm.
    - The students should draw the forms accurately with lead pencil. Certain aspects of the form can be accentuated with color pencils and shadings; beauty and exactness are important. However, any artwork or shading should be simple, with the purpose of bringing out the most important characteristics of the form.
    - Some of the drawings can be done on larger pieces of paper.
    - The use of the geometric tools (compass and straightedge) should wait until the sixth grade during the *Geometric Drawing* main lesson.
    - There are many wonderful ideas for freehand geometry in Ernst Schuberth's book, *Geometry Lessons in the Waldorf School, Volume 2*. However, note that we recommend freehand geometry in fifth grade, and geometric drawing (with compass and straightedge) for sixth grade, whereas Schuberth lists both of these for a year earlier.
  - Area and perimeter of rectangles and squares can now be introduced.
  - *Pythagorean Theorem.*
    - Since ancient Greek history and culture is a theme of fifth grade, we can tell Pythagoras's biography and introduce his theorem. (See Julia Diggins' book, page 92-105.)
    - By giving an artistic introduction to the Pythagorean Theorem in fifth grade, we are planting a seed for geometry in the upper grades. Connection with will and feeling is important. Be sure not to make it too intellectual.
    - The Pythagorean Theorem is an important mathematical law. The children's first experience with it should be artistic and very hands-on. We are simply playing with the theorem; the intellectual concept is not yet introduced. (See the sample drawing of this on our website.)
- *The Wonder of Number.*
  - Important!! There are many ideas given below (under *More Ideas for Teaching Fifth Grade Math*) for what could be brought to the class during this main lesson. Some of the possible topics are: *Square and Triangular Numbers, Powers of Two, Divisibility Rules, Perfect Numbers, Sum and Difference Theorems*. These are all just ideas. None of it is compulsory. Whatever isn't covered in fifth grade could be covered at any point in grades six through eight, or not covered at all.
  - This is a truly wonderful main lesson to bring to the children as long as the teacher has the time and desire to learn and penetrate the material sufficiently. The teacher needs to find an appropriate and creative way to bring it to the children.
  - It is important that the students discover for themselves the properties of numbers described below, or, at least, that the students come to some understanding of where they come from. We should not just give the numbers and properties to them. Wonder arises from discovery!
- *Don't forget to review and practice – 30 minutes per day during a math main lesson!* Material that has been introduced in previous blocks and in previous years needs to be reviewed, practiced, and furthered. (See above *Practice and review of old material under Lessons and Topics for Fifth Grade*.)

Fifth Grade Math

<u>Movement and manipulatives</u>
- The Pythagorean Theorem can be cut out and glued.
  (Visit our website **www.JamieYorkPress.com** to see full-color drawings of this.)
- Many movement exercises can be done outside, such as:
  - The students can move their arms to represent different angles.
  - The class can form a circle with one student at the center and everyone else an equal distance from the center person.
  - In a similar way, the class can form different triangles, angles, squares, parallel lines. etc.
- *Making A Right Angle with a Rope.*
  - The following is an example of how the Egyptians were able to make a right angle by using a rope.
    - Bring the class into a field and have a rope that is 120 feet long, with a knot tied 50 feet from one end and 40 feet from the other end. (The distance between the two knots should now be 30 feet.) Form a triangle with the rope, such that the three corners of the triangle are the two knots and the place where the ends of the rope come together. All three sides of the triangle should be tight and straight. The result should be a right triangle.
    - You should show that if one knot is moved a few feet, then you no longer get a right angle.

<u>Bookwork</u>
- After practicing each geometric form on loose drawing paper, each form should be drawn beautifully in the main lesson book.
- Be sure to visit our website (**www.JamieYorkPress.com**) to see full-color pages from students' main lesson books.

Fifth Grade Math

More Ideas for Teaching Fifth Grade Math
Wonder of Number

(Be sure to reread the section, *Thoughts on Teaching Math in the Lower Grades*, found at the start of this book.)

Note: This entire section (4 pages) is intended for the *Wonder of Number* main lesson block. None of it is compulsory. Whatever isn't covered in fifth grade, could be covered at any point in grades six through eight, or not covered at all. A good amount of what is listed here is for the teacher's curiosity and interest. It should only be brought into the classroom if the teacher has adequately penetrated the material, and can find an appropriate and creative way to bring it to the children.

Square and Triangular Numbers

- See Appendix, *Square and Triangular Numbers,* for a listing of the square and triangular numbers.
- *The square numbers* are 1, 4, 9, 16, etc.
    - They are found by squaring each whole number: $1^2, 2^2, 3^2, 4^2$, etc.
    - They can be geometrically made into squares by placing dots into square shapes: three rows of three make 9, four rows of four make 16, etc., as shown below.
    - Alternatively, they can also be found by adding sequences of odd numbers. For example, the fourth square number can be found by adding the first four odd numbers: 1+3+5+7, which is 16. Similarly, the sixth square number can be found by adding the first six odd numbers: 1+3+5+7+9+11, which is 36.

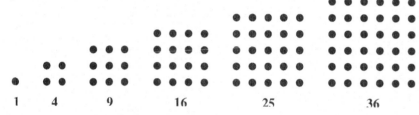

- *The triangular numbers* are 1, 3, 6, 10, 15, 21, 28, 36, etc.
    - The reason that they are called triangular can be explained by looking at the way that the dots are placed in a triangular form, as shown below.

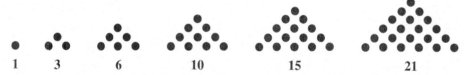

    - The triangular numbers can be found by adding a sequence of numbers. For example, the fourth triangular number is found by adding the first four numbers: 1+2+3+4, which is 10. Similarly, the sixth triangular number is found by adding 1+2+3+4+5+6, which is 21.

- *A neat theorem!* The sum of two consecutive triangular numbers is a square number. A nice "proof" of this is shown with the drawing here. This can be quite a thrill for students to discover on their own!

- Have the students try to find the first three numbers that are *both* square and triangular. There are only seven numbers below 2 billion that are *both* square and triangular. They are

    1   36   1225   41,616   1,413,721   48,024,900   1,631,432,881

Powers of two (See *Powers of Two Table* in the appendix.)

- We can ask the children: What do we get if we multiply two 2's together? How about multiplying three 2's together? And ten 2's? And twenty 2's? They may be surprised how the results get large very quickly.
- It may be best to not introduce notation that uses exponents until sixth grade.

Fifth Grade Math

Divisibility Rules

- A number is evenly <u>divisible by 10</u> (i.e., can be divided by 10 with no remainder) only if the number ends in a 0.
- A number is evenly <u>divisible by 5</u> only if the number ends in a 5 or a 0.
- A number is evenly <u>divisible by 2</u> only if it is even.
- A number is evenly <u>divisible by 4</u> only if the last two digits are divisible by 4.
  This is particularly fun for the children because someone can give them any large number and they only have to listen for the last two digits in order to determine if the number is evenly divisible by 4. The students can then try to figure out how to do this quickly in the case that the last two digits are greater than 50. One method is to subtract 20, 40, 60 or 80 in order to make it easier.
  - *Example*: Is 6,380,716 evenly divisible by 4?
    Solution: We see that it ends in 16, which is evenly divisible by 4. Therefore, 6,380,716 is also evenly divisible by 4.
  - *Example*: Is 98,273,474 evenly divisible by 4?
    Solution: We see that it ends in 74. We subtract 60, leaving us with 14, which isn't evenly divisible by 4. Therefore, 98,273,474 is *not* evenly divisible by 4.
- A number is evenly <u>divisible by 3</u> only if the sum of the digits is divisible by 3.
  For example, for 71,284 we add up the digits to get 22. Because 22 is not divisible by 3, we can conclude that 71,284 is not evenly divisible by 3.
- A number is evenly <u>divisible by 9</u> only if the sum of the digits is divisible by 9.

Perfect, Abundant, and Deficient Numbers

- See Appendix, *Perfect, Abundant, and Deficient Numbers,* for a listing of these numbers.
- The Greeks (especially the Pythagoreans) believed that certain numbers had special meaning and significance. They studied perfect, abundant, and deficient numbers in detail.
- *What are perfect, abundant, and deficient numbers?* In general, a whole number is categorized as abundant, deficient or perfect based upon the sum of its factors. In order to determine whether a given whole number is perfect, abundant or deficient, we first list all the number's factors, <u>except for the number itself</u>. Then we sum up the numbers in that list. If this sum is equal to the number itself, then we say that the number is *perfect*. If this sum is less than the number itself, then we say that the number is *deficient*. If the sum is greater than the number itself, then we say that the number is *abundant*.
- *Discovering Perfect Numbers*. Show the students that 10 is a *deficient number* because the sum of its factors (1, 2, 5) is less than 10. Then show the students that 20 is an *abundant number* because the sum of its factors (1, 2, 4, 5, 10) is greater than 20. Then tell the students that there are only two *perfect numbers* under 100, and let them try to find these two special numbers. (They are 6 and 28.)
- *More perfect numbers?* Perfect numbers are extremely rare; there are only four perfect numbers below 10,000,000. The students now know that the first two perfect numbers are 6 and 28, and that the next perfect number is greater than 100. You can then mention that the third perfect number is less than 1000, and the fourth one is less than 10,000. Tell them that they will have to wait until seventh grade to learn how to calculate these perfect numbers. (A bit of drama never hurt!)
- *The abundance quotient* is the quotient that results when the sum of factors (without the number itself) is divided by the number itself.

  Example: Determine whether the number 10 is perfect, abundant or deficient, and calculate its abundance quotient.
  Solution: The list of factors for 10 is 1, 2, 5. The sum of these factors is 8, which is less than the number itself (10), so the number is *deficient*. The abundance quotient is 8÷10, which is <u>0.8</u>.

  Example: Determine whether the number 20 is perfect, abundant or deficient, and calculate its abundance quotient.
  Solution: The list of factors for 20 is 1, 2, 4, 5, 10. The sum of these factors is 22, which is greater than the number itself (20), so the number is *abundant*. The abundance quotient is 22÷20, which is <u>1.1</u>.

Fifth Grade Math

Example: Determine whether the number 28 is perfect, abundant or deficient, and calculate its abundance quotient.

Solution: The list of factors for 28 is 1, 2, 4, 7, 14. The sum of these factors is 28, which is equal to the number itself (28), so the number is *perfect*. The abundance quotient (for all perfect numbers) is exactly <u>1</u>.

- *More about perfect, abundant, and deficient numbers* (for the teacher).
  - There are 21 even abundant numbers under 100. The first odd abundant number is 945.
  - The first 7 perfect numbers[34] are:
    6; 28; 496; 8128; 33,550,336; 8,589,869,056; 137,438,691,328.
  - Early on, the Greeks knew that the first three perfect numbers were 6, 28, and 496. They had troubles finding perfect numbers beyond that because the numbers were getting too large to list and add all the factors. They wanted to find an easier method for determining perfect numbers.
  - Euclid discovered a formula for calculating even perfect numbers around 300B.C. This formula (See *A Source Book for Teaching Middle School Math, A Middle School Math Curriculum*, under seventh grade algebra) made it possible to discover the next few perfect numbers (perhaps up to the seventh one). In the 1600's, Jean Prestet found the eighth perfect number: 2,305,843,008,139,952,128.
  - There are no known odd perfect numbers, and it is one of the great mysteries of mathematics whether or not an odd perfect number could possibly exist.

Sum and Difference Theorems

- Each of the below theorems expresses some surprising law about the relationship of numbers. If properly brought to the children, this can engender a real sense of wonder. It should only be brought to the children if the teacher has developed a good connection to this material.
- The challenge is to not make it too abstract. Try to make it playful.
- The Greeks were very interested in how numbers could be expressed as the sum or difference of other special numbers (e.g., prime numbers or square numbers). It was the famous French mathematician, Pierre de Fermat, who, around 1640, came up with the below theorems (except for the first one).
- *Goldbach's Conjecture*: "*Every even number can be expressed as the sum of two prime numbers.*"
  - Simply ask the children how many ways they can find to express 90 as the sum of two prime numbers. Have them list the different possibilities that they have found on the board. They will be amazed to see that there are nine ways to express 90 as the sum of two primes (7+83; 11+79; 17+73; 19+71; 23+67; 29+61; 31+59; 37+53; 43+47).
  - In contrast, there are only two ways to express 68 as the sum of two primes (7+61 and 31+37).
  - Once we get past the first few even numbers, most all of them can be expressed as the sum of two prime numbers in multiple ways, yet the number of possible ways varies greatly.
  - While most mathematicians believe that this theorem is true, nobody has been able to prove it (but many have tried!).
  - See Appendix, *Even Numbers as the Sum of Two Primes,* for a list of all the ways that the even numbers from 4 to 150 can be expressed as the sum of two primes.
- *The difference of two square numbers.*

  "*Every prime number, except for 2, can be expressed as the difference of two square numbers in one and only one way.*"
  - The students should first make a list of consecutive square numbers:
    1 4 9 16 25 36...   We see that the differences/distances grow.
      3 5 7 9 11...   ← These are the differences between neighbors.

  Given that the above differences between neighbors form the list of odd numbers, we can easily see how *any odd number can be expressed as the difference of two squares*. For example, we can

---

[34] Note that "1" is not considered to be a perfect number for the same reason that it isn't considered to be a prime number: it is the basis of all numbers. Also, our list of factors isn't supposed to include the number itself, so the number 1 doesn't have any numbers in its list of factors.

express 7 as 16−9 (which is $4^2 - 3^2$). Similarly, we can express 15 as 64 − 49 (which is $8^2 - 7^2$).

The real surprise with the above theorem is that it says, if the odd number is a prime number, then it can be expressed as a difference of two squares in *only one way*. For example, 15 can be expressed as the difference of two squares *in two ways*: either as $8^2 - 7^2$ or as $4^2 - 1^2$. This does not contradict our theorem because 15 is not a prime number. 7, on the other hand, is prime, so we know that it can only be expressed as $4^2 - 3^2$.

- See Appendix, *Odd Numbers as the Difference of Two Squares*, for a list of all the ways that the odd numbers from 3 to 299 can be expressed as the *difference* of two squares.

- *The sum of two square numbers.*

"If a number is prime and has a remainder of 1 after dividing it by 4, then it can be expressed as the sum of two square numbers in one and only one way."
  - The number 73 is both prime and has a remainder of 1 when divided by 4. This theorem tells us that there must be exactly one way to express 73 as the sum of two squares. Looking in the appendix at *Numbers as the Sum of Two Squares*, we see that 73 can be expressed only as $8^2 + 3^2$.
  - See Appendix, *Numbers as the Sum of Two Squares*, for a list of all the ways that the numbers from 2 to 442 can be expressed as the *sum* of two squares.

"If a number is prime and has a remainder of 3 after dividing it by 4, then it is not possible to express it as a sum of two square numbers."
  - The number 43 is both prime and has a remainder of 3 when divided by 4. The theorem says that it must be impossible to express 43 as the sum of two squares. Looking in the appendix at *Numbers as the Sum of Two Squares* confirms that 43 can't be expressed as the sum of two squares.

"If a number is not prime, then there are a variety of possibilities – it may be that the number can be expressed as the sum of two square numbers in one way, in multiple ways, or not at all."
  - Looking in the appendix at *Numbers as the Sum of Two Squares*, we can see the following:
    - 45 can be expressed as the sum of two squares in exactly one way: $6^2 + 3^2$.
    - 48 can't be expressed as the sum of two squares in any way.
    - 50 is the first number that can be expressed as the sum of two squares in 2 ways:
      $5^2 + 5^2$ or $7^2 + 1^2$
    - 325 is the first number that can be expressed as the sum of two squares in 3 ways:
      $1^2 + 18^2$; $6^2 + 17^2$; $10^2 + 15^2$
    - 1105 is the first number that can be expressed as the sum of two squares in 4 ways:
      $4^2 + 33^2$; $9^2 + 32^2$; $12^2 + 31^2$; $23^2 + 24^2$

Fermat's Little Theorem
- Let X be equal to 2. Choose any number (but don't make it too big!), and call it "Q". Calculate x^Q (which will need to be explained to the children without using exponent notation). Take this result and subtract X from it – the result we will call "D". Here is the question: Is D evenly divisible by Q? The children should then try a variety of possible values for Q, from Q=2 all the way up to Q=15. What patterns do we notice?
- Ultimately, we want to answer this question: "By just looking at the value of Q, how can we predict whether D will be evenly divisible by Q?" The answer is *Fermat's Little Theorem*: "If Q is a prime number, then D will always be evenly divisible by Q." And X can also be anything other than 2.[35]

---

[35] It would also seem that if Q is composite (i.e., not prime) then D won't be evenly divisible by Q. If X = 2, all of the composite numbers that we could reasonably try would support this statement. But, quite surprisingly, if we let Q=341 (which is evenly divisible by 11), then the resulting 103-digit value for D turns out to be evenly divisible by 341. If X is greater than 2, then generally we can easily find composite values for Q that divide evenly into D.

Appendix

Appendix

A Math Curriculum Summary for Grades One through Five

— First Grade —

The world of numbers.
- Roman numerals. Begin with the Roman numerals, and then move into the (standard) Arabic numbers.
- Quality of numbers. What is the quality of the numbers in the surrounding world?
- Counting. Counting forward and backward to 100, with ease. Awaken a sense for number.
- Number dictations. There should be number dictations starting in the second math block.

Developing a sense of numbers.
- Rhythmical counting. Rhythmical counting serves as preparation for learning the times tables later.
- Movement. The challenge is to synchronize the movement with the speaking voice.
- Estimating. "How many steps am I from the board?"

Beginning calculations.
- Introducing the four processes. The children become at ease with adding and subtracting numbers up to 24, and fluently up to 10.
- Regrouping numbers. For example, how can we regroup the number ten?
- Learning the "easy" addition facts. All addition facts up to 10, as well as all of the doubles (i.e., 6+6, 7+7, 8+8, 9+9) should be learned by heart by the end of first grade.

— Second Grade —

The world of numbers The students should become at ease with the number world up to 1000 (and beyond?).

Estimating. We build up from the estimating done in first grade and progress to more challenging estimations.

Place value. Place value should be introduced and practiced. This is an important step.

Addition and subtraction facts. By the end of the year, the class should learn *by heart* their addition facts (up to 24) and the corresponding subtraction facts. They should also be at ease with addition and subtraction up to 100.

The times/division tables. By the end of the year, the class should be comfortable with all of the times and division tables from 1-12, in a row. This requires daily, systematic work!

The four processes.
- *Addition.* By the end of the year, the class should be *at ease* with adding any two-digit number with a one-digit number (e.g., 57+6).
- *Subtraction.* By the end of the year, the class should be *at ease* with subtracting any one-digit number from a two-digit number (e.g., 52–6), and also with subtracting two 2-digit numbers such that the answer is a one-digit number (e.g., 72–69).
- The students must gain an understanding of the concept of multiplication and division, such as:
    $3 \times 2 = 6$ means "three groups of two make six".
    $12 \div 3 = 4$ means "how many groups of three fit in twelve?"
- By the end of the year, the children should be able to do all four processes (even alternating on the same page) and know the difference between the processes without help. But keep the problems simple!

Time orientation. The days of the week and the months of the year.

The wonder of number. Geometrical patterns that arise from the times/division tables and the circle.

Appendix

— Third Grade —

The world of numbers. Fluent up to 1000 and at ease with the numbers up into the millions.

Learning all of the arithmetic facts!! Now is the time to learn the multiplication and division facts (that come from these tables) out of order, as well as all of the addition facts and subtraction facts. Systematic daily work, both orally and written (e.g., with our *arithmetic fact practice sheets*) is needed.

The four processes – working vertically.
- An introduction to vertical addition ("carrying") and vertical subtraction ("borrowing"). Build up to adding two 4-digit numbers (e.g., 8364+8375) and subtracting two 3-digit numbers (e.g., 643–387).
- An introduction to vertical multiplication. Only do single-digit multipliers (e.g., 2347x5).
- An introduction to vertical (long) division may be delayed until fourth grade. If done in third grade, only do two-step problems with divisors from 1-12 (e.g., 332÷4).

The four processes – working horizontally. Even though the children are being introduced to working with the four processes in vertical form, the bulk of their work with the four processes is still in horizontal form.

Measurement. Introduction to time, distance, weight, and volume.

— Fourth Grade —

The world of numbers. GCF (greatest common factor) and LCM (least common multiple).

The arithmetic facts. Continued work both orally and written (e.g., with our *arithmetic fact review sheets*).

The four processes. Regular practice is needed.
- *Horizontal addition and subtraction.* Problems like: 125+126, 895 + 112, 974 – 875.
- *Vertical addition and subtraction.* Work with larger numbers than what was done in third grade.
- *Vertical multiplication.* We can build up to three-digit multipliers (e.g., 4372x836).
- *Vertical (long) division.* Whether this is introduced in third or fourth grade, we now build up to four-step problems, but the divisors should still be kept between 1 and 12 (e.g., 15288÷6=2548).

Fractions. An introduction to fractions, including: types of fractions, equivalent fractions, and simple arithmetic with fractions. The goal is to get to the end of fourth grade with the class having a good understanding of the basics of fractions, and having the children saying, "I like fractions!"

Measurement. Review third grade measurement, and begin doing simple conversion problems.

— Fifth Grade —

Fractions. The students should become fluent in working with common denominators and at ease with unlike denominators. Multiplying and dividing of common fractions should be thoroughly practiced.

Decimal fractions. The number world of decimal fractions is introduced.

Measurement. The metric system (distance, weight, and capacity) is introduced. Review of the U.S. system is integrated into our work with the metric system.

Geometry.
- *Freehand geometry.* The students create many beautiful drawings of circles, squares, triangles, angles, divisions of the circle, etc., all freehand, without the aid of a ruler or compass.
- We can bring an imaginative picture of the *Pythagorean Theorem*.
- We can also introduce *perimeter and area*.

The Wonder of Number. Some of the possible topics are: *Square and Triangular Numbers, Powers of Two, Divisibility Rules, Perfect Numbers,* and *Sum and Difference Theorems.* Leave them in wonder!

Review and Practice. It is especially important to review (and further) all work with vertical arithmetic (addition, subtraction, long multiplication, and long division), and all work with fractions.

Arithmetic facts. Review and practice of the arithmetic facts is still important. This can be done a couple of times per week both orally and written (e.g., with our *arithmetic fact speed sheets*).

Appendix

A List of Games for Lower Grades Math

Notes:
- All of the following games[36] are related to math.
- It is fun for the students to experience the world of numbers in a playful way.
- All these games can be used from grade two and up.

Our puzzle and game book
- There may be times when the teacher knows it is time to do something different. Our *Making Math Meaningful Puzzle and Game Book* is intended as a resource for math teachers in grades four through twelve, in part to supplement the normal classroom material. It provides ideas for that "something different". It can ordered through our website **www.JamieYorkPress.com**.

Dominoes games (there is a great variety)
- Krypto Card Games
- Numbers Factory

Bingo games (there is a great variety)
- Conceptual Bingo with Fractions
- Conceptual Bingo with Decimals
- Conceptual Bingo with Fractions to Decimals

Traditional games (that can help with simple counting, and arithmetic)
- Monopoly
- Yahtzee
- Shut the Box
- Can't Stop

Games using the four processes (+,−,x,÷)
- Equate (All Star Math games)
- Roll 'n Multiply (All Star Math games)
- Smath: The Game That Makes Math Fun.
- Hands on Learning, math card games
- Math Mania Highlights

Other ideas
- A Box with Six Math Board Games for all Ages
- Mind Bending Puzzles Books, by Lagoon Books
- Books with Mazes
- Books with Patterns

---

[36] Most of these games were found at the store "Math and Stuff" in Seattle. It is a wellspring of math resources. Visit their website at www.math-n-stuff.com.

Appendix
A Step-by-Step Progression for the Arithmetic Facts

Step #1: *Basic rhythmical counting* (first grade).
In first grade, rhythmical counting exercises are done with the 2's, 3's, 4's, 5's, 10's, and 11's tables.

Step #2: *Addition and subtraction facts* (first and second grade).
Starting in first grade with some of the more basic facts (e.g., 5=3+2, and 12=6+6), the children begin to learn the addition facts, and corresponding subtraction facts, by heart. By the end of second grade, these more basic facts should be solid with most of the students, and by the end of third grade, the whole class should have mastered all of the addition and subtraction facts.

Step #3: *Basic times/division tables* (second grade) – the 2's, 3's, 4's, 5's, 10's, and 11's tables.
We now build on the rhythmical counting exercises that were done in first grade. In second grade, we begin to introduce the times/division tables as a concept, in an artistic way. These are introduced through movement in different ways and also written down. We should find ways to integrate the times and division tables together. For example, we can say:
1x6=6, 6=1x6, 6÷1=6;
2x6=12, 12=2x6, 12÷2=6;
3x6=18, 18=3x6, 18÷3=6, etc.

Step #4: *Advanced times/division tables* (second grade) – the 6's, 7's, 8's, and 9's tables.
In first grade, rhythmical counting exercises were not done for 6 through 9. Now in second grade, they can work on the 6's table through the 9's table, and the 12's table as well. As opposed to the rhythmical counting that was done in first grade, the class can jump right into speaking each of these more advanced tables (e.g., with the 6's, we say: "6, 12, 18, 24, 30, etc.").

Step #5: *Individual practice!* (second grade).
First, after a times table has been introduced and we have practiced the rhythmical sequences of that times table, we then need to have the children practice writing the times and division tables in a row. Each student should be able to write down each times table in a horizontal row without any help.

Step #6: *Arithmetic facts* (third grade).
The goal is that, by the end of third grade, the whole class has learned the arithmetic facts by heart. Our *arithmetic facts practice sheets* are designed to be done almost daily for 20 weeks. (For more details, see *All about the Third Grade Arithmetic Facts Practice Sheets* under *More Ideas for Teaching Third Grade Math*.) In third grade, we should also work with remainders (e.g., 20÷6 = 3 r 2).

Step #7: *Review and practice* (fourth and fifth grade).
Arithmetic facts practice, review and speed sheets should be done in fourth and fifth grade in order to reinforce what has been learned, and to keep it fresh. Two or three sheets per week – each sheet taking only 3-5 minutes – should be enough. Daily mental arithmetic also supports this effort.

Additional notes on learning the arithmetic facts

- There may be a significant overlap between some of the above steps – i.e., one step does not necessarily need to be finished with all tables before beginning the next step with another table.

- Rhythmical work should continue in third grade, but we must ensure that it includes sufficient work with the "head memory". To do this effectively, we shouldn't only have the students recite the tables together as a class with choral speaking, but we should also call on individual students to give answers to facts out of sequence.

- *The multiplication facts* aren't so numerous. There are a total of 66 multiplication facts, but only 17 of them are "hard" (these are from the 6's, 7's, 8's, 9's and 12's, tables, plus 11x11 and 11x12). Even if you add in the 4's and 3's tables, that's only 30 "hard" facts to learn.

- *Division facts.* Starting in second grade, the division facts should always be done with the multiplication facts. For instance, if you are working on 8x7=56, then at the same time you can do 56÷8, and 56÷7, as well as problems like 8 x __ = 56.

- *Subtraction facts.*
  - The subtraction facts are often not given enough emphasis. In middle school, it is often the subtraction facts (e.g., 12–7) that slow students down the most when doing calculations.
  - There are 81 subtraction facts to memorize – 45 subtraction facts that are from 10 and under (e.g., 8–3) and 36 "borrowing" facts (e.g., 13–8). Practicing the subtraction facts in first through third grade is very important.

Appendix

The First 100 Square Numbers

```
#1  is  1         #26 is  676      #51 is 2601      #76  is 5776
#2  is  4         #27 is  729      #52 is 2704      #77  is 5929
#3  is  9         #28 is  784      #53 is 2809      #78  is 6084
#4  is  16        #29 is  841      #54 is 2916      #79  is 6241
#5  is  25        #30 is  900      #55 is 3025      #80  is 6400
#6  is  36        #31 is  961      #56 is 3136      #81  is 6561
#7  is  49        #32 is 1024      #57 is 3249      #82  is 6724
#8  is  64        #33 is 1089      #58 is 3364      #83  is 6889
#9  is  81        #34 is 1156      #59 is 3481      #84  is 7056
#10 is  100       #35 is 1225      #60 is 3600      #85  is 7225
#11 is  121       #36 is 1296      #61 is 3721      #86  is 7396
#12 is  144       #37 is 1369      #62 is 3844      #87  is 7569
#13 is  169       #38 is 1444      #63 is 3969      #88  is 7744
#14 is  196       #39 is 1521      #64 is 4096      #89  is 7921
#15 is  225       #40 is 1600      #65 is 4225      #90  is 8100
#16 is  256       #41 is 1681      #66 is 4356      #91  is 8281
#17 is  289       #42 is 1764      #67 is 4489      #92  is 8464
#18 is  324       #43 is 1849      #68 is 4624      #93  is 8649
#19 is  361       #44 is 1936      #69 is 4761      #94  is 8836
#20 is  400       #45 is 2025      #70 is 4900      #95  is 9025
#21 is  441       #46 is 2116      #71 is 5041      #96  is 9216
#22 is  484       #47 is 2209      #72 is 5184      #97  is 9409
#23 is  529       #48 is 2304      #73 is 5329      #98  is 9604
#24 is  576       #49 is 2401      #74 is 5476      #99  is 9801
#25 is  625       #50 is 2500      #75 is 5625      #100 is 10000
```

The First 75 Triangular Numbers

```
#1  is  1         #20 is 210       #39 is  780      #58 is 1711
#2  is  3         #21 is 231       #40 is  820      #59 is 1770
#3  is  6         #22 is 253       #41 is  861      #60 is 1830
#4  is  10        #23 is 276       #42 is  903      #61 is 1891
#5  is  15        #24 is 300       #43 is  946      #62 is 1953
#6  is  21        #25 is 325       #44 is  990      #63 is 2016
#7  is  28        #26 is 351       #45 is 1035      #64 is 2080
#8  is  36        #27 is 378       #46 is 1081      #65 is 2145
#9  is  45        #28 is 406       #47 is 1128      #66 is 2211
#10 is  55        #29 is 435       #48 is 1176      #67 is 2278
#11 is  66        #30 is 465       #49 is 1225      #68 is 2346
#12 is  78        #31 is 496       #50 is 1275      #69 is 2415
#13 is  91        #32 is 528       #51 is 1326      #70 is 2485
#14 is  105       #33 is 561       #52 is 1378      #71 is 2556
#15 is  120       #34 is 595       #53 is 1431      #72 is 2628
#16 is  136       #35 is 630       #54 is 1485      #73 is 2701
#17 is  153       #36 is 666       #55 is 1540      #74 is 2775
#18 is  171       #37 is 703       #56 is 1596      #75 is 2850
#19 is  190       #38 is 741       #57 is 1653
```

Appendix

Perfect, Abundant, and Deficient Numbers

The abundance quotient is the sum of its factors (except for the number itself) divided by the number itself. For example, with 24, the sum of its factors is 36, so the abundance quotient for 24 is 36÷24 = 1.5.

All perfect numbers, by definition, have an abundance quotient exactly equal to one. The first nine perfect numbers are:

6	8,589,869,056
28	137,438,691,328
496	2,305,843,008,139,952,128
8128	2,658,455,991,569,831,744,654,692,615,953,842,176.
33,550,336	

The tenth perfect number has 54 digits! It is still unknown if any odd perfect number exists.

Interestingly, the first 231 abundant numbers are all even numbers. The first odd-numbered abundant number is 945 (quotient = 1.032), and the second one is 1575 (quotient = 1.047). The *abundance quotients* of each of the "biggest" abundant numbers (i.e., having an abundance quotient greater than any previous number) from 6 up to 30,000 are listed below.

12 is abundant with a quotient of 1.333	720 is abundant with a quotient of 2.358
24 is abundant with a quotient of 1.500	840 is abundant with a quotient of 2.429
36 is abundant with a quotient of 1.528	1260 is abundant with a quotient of 2.467
48 is abundant with a quotient of 1.583	1680 is abundant with a quotient of 2.543
60 is abundant with a quotient of 1.800	2520 is abundant with a quotient of 2.714
120 is abundant with a quotient of 2.000	5040 is abundant with a quotient of 2.838
180 is abundant with a quotient of 2.033	10080 is abundant with a quotient of 2.900
240 is abundant with a quotient of 2.100	15120 is abundant with a quotient of 2.937
360 is abundant with a quotient of 2.250	25200 is abundant with a quotient of 2.966
	27720 is abundant with a quotient of 3.052

Here are the abundance quotients for the abundant numbers up to 150:

```
12  has a quotient of  1.333      80  has a quotient of  1.325
18  has a quotient of  1.167      84  has a quotient of  1.667
20  has a quotient of  1.100      88  has a quotient of  1.045
24  has a quotient of  1.500      90  has a quotient of  1.600
28  has a quotient of  1.000      96  has a quotient of  1.625
30  has a quotient of  1.400     100  has a quotient of  1.170
36  has a quotient of  1.528     102  has a quotient of  1.118
40  has a quotient of  1.250     104  has a quotient of  1.019
42  has a quotient of  1.286     108  has a quotient of  1.593
48  has a quotient of  1.583     112  has a quotient of  1.214
54  has a quotient of  1.222     114  has a quotient of  1.105
56  has a quotient of  1.143     120  has a quotient of  2.000
60  has a quotient of  1.800     126  has a quotient of  1.476
66  has a quotient of  1.182     132  has a quotient of  1.545
70  has a quotient of  1.057     138  has a quotient of  1.087
72  has a quotient of  1.708     140  has a quotient of  1.400
78  has a quotient of  1.154
```

Appendix

Powers of Two Table

2 to the 1 is 2
2 to the 2 is 4
2 to the 3 is 8
2 to the 4 is 16
2 to the 5 is 32
2 to the 6 is 64
2 to the 7 is 128
2 to the 8 is 256
2 to the 9 is 512
2 to the 10 is 1,024
2 to the 11 is 2,048
2 to the 12 is 4,096
2 to the 13 is 8,192
2 to the 14 is 16,384
2 to the 15 is 32,768
2 to the 16 is 65,536
2 to the 17 is 131,072
2 to the 18 is 262,144
2 to the 19 is 524,288
2 to the 20 is 1,048,576
2 to the 21 is 2,097,152
2 to the 22 is 4,194,304
2 to the 23 is 8,388,608
2 to the 24 is 16,777,216
2 to the 25 is 33,554,432
2 to the 26 is 67,108,864
2 to the 27 is 134,217,728
2 to the 28 is 268,435,456
2 to the 29 is 536,870,912
2 to the 30 is 1,073,741,824
2 to the 31 is 2,147,483,648
2 to the 32 is 4,294,967,296
2 to the 33 is 8,589,934,592
2 to the 34 is 17,179,869,184
2 to the 35 is 34,359,738,368
2 to the 36 is 68,719,476,736
2 to the 37 is 137,438,953,472
2 to the 38 is 274,877,906,944
2 to the 39 is 549,755,813,888
2 to the 40 is 1,099,511,627,776
2 to the 41 is 2,199,023,255,552
2 to the 42 is 4,398,046,511,104
2 to the 43 is 8,796,093,022,208
2 to the 44 is 17,592,186,044,416
2 to the 45 is 35,184,372,088,832
2 to the 46 is 70,368,744,177,664
2 to the 47 is 140,737,488,355,328
2 to the 48 is 281,474,976,710,656
2 to the 49 is 562,949,953,421,312
2 to the 50 is 1,125,899,906,842,624

2 to the 51 is 2,251,799,813,685,248
2 to the 52 is 4,503,599,627,370,496
2 to the 53 is 9,007,199,254,740,992
2 to the 54 is 18,014,398,509,481,984
2 to the 55 is 36,028,797,018,963,968
2 to the 56 is 72,057,594,037,927,936
2 to the 57 is 144,115,188,075,855,872
2 to the 58 is 288,230,376,151,711,744
2 to the 59 is 576,460,752,303,423,488
2 to the 60 is 1,152,921,504,606,846,976
2 to the 61 is 2,305,843,009,213,693,952
2 to the 62 is 4,611,686,018,427,387,904
2 to the 63 is 9,223,372,036,854,775,808
2 to the 64 is 18,446,744,073,709,551,616
2 to the 65 is 36,893,488,147,419,103,232
2 to the 66 is 73,786,976,294,838,206,464
2 to the 67 is 147,573,952,589,676,412,928
2 to the 68 is 295,147,905,179,352,825,856
2 to the 69 is 590,295,810,358,705,651,712
2 to the 70 is 1,180,591,620,717,411,303,424
2 to the 71 is 2,361,183,241,434,822,606,848
2 to the 72 is 4,722,366,482,869,645,213,696
2 to the 73 is 9,444,732,965,739,290,427,392
2 to the 74 is 18,889,465,931,478,580,854,784
2 to the 75 is 37,778,931,862,957,161,709,568
2 to the 76 is 75,557,863,725,914,323,419,136
2 to the 77 is 151,115,727,451,828,646,838,272
2 to the 78 is 302,231,454,903,657,293,676,544
2 to the 79 is 604,462,909,807,314,587,353,088
2 to the 80 is 1,208,925,819,614,629,174,706,176
2 to the 81 is 2,417,851,639,229,258,349,412,352
2 to the 82 is 4,835,703,278,458,516,698,824,704
2 to the 83 is 9,671,406,556,917,033,397,649,408
2 to the 84 is 19,342,813,113,834,066,795,298,816
2 to the 85 is 38,685,626,227,668,133,590,597,632
2 to the 86 is 77,371,252,455,336,267,181,195,264
2 to the 87 is 154,742,504,910,672,534,362,390,528
2 to the 88 is 309,485,009,821,345,068,724,781,056
2 to the 89 is 618,970,019,642,690,137,449,562,112
2 to the 90 is 1,237,940,039,285,380,274,899,124,224
2 to the 91 is 2,475,880,078,570,760,549,798,248,448
2 to the 92 is 4,951,760,157,141,521,099,596,496,896
2 to the 93 is 9,903,520,314,283,042,199,192,993,792
2 to the 94 is 19,807,040,628,566,084,398,385,987,584
2 to the 95 is 39,614,081,257,132,168,796,771,975,168
2 to the 96 is 79,228,162,514,264,337,593,543,950,336
2 to the 97 is 158,456,325,028,528,675,187,087,900,672
2 to the 98 is 316,912,650,057,057,350,374,175,801,344
2 to the 99 is 633,825,300,114,114,700,748,351,602,688
2 to the 100 is 1,267,650,600,228,229,401,496,703,205,376

Appendix

Prime Numbers up to 2000 (in groups of 250)

2	251	503	751	1009	1259	1511	1753
3	257	509	757	1013	1277	1523	1759
5	263	521	761	1019	1279	1531	1777
7	269	523	769	1021	1283	1543	1783
11	271	541	773	1031	1289	1549	1787
13	277	547	787	1033	1291	1553	1789
17	281	557	797	1039	1297	1559	1801
19	283	563	809	1049	1301	1567	1811
23	293	569	811	1051	1303	1571	1823
29	307	571	821	1061	1307	1579	1831
31	311	577	823	1063	1319	1583	1847
37	313	587	827	1069	1321	1597	1861
41	317	593	829	1087	1327	1601	1867
43	331	599	839	1091	1361	1607	1871
47	337	601	853	1093	1367	1609	1873
53	347	607	857	1097	1373	1613	1877
59	349	613	859	1103	1381	1619	1879
61	353	617	863	1109	1399	1621	1889
67	359	619	877	1117	1409	1627	1901
71	367	631	881	1123	1423	1637	1907
73	373	641	883	1129	1427	1657	1913
79	379	643	887	1151	1429	1663	1931
83	383	647	907	1153	1433	1667	1933
89	389	653	911	1163	1439	1669	1949
97	397	659	919	1171	1447	1693	1951
101	401	661	929	1181	1451	1697	1973
103	409	673	937	1187	1453	1699	1979
107	419	677	941	1193	1459	1709	1987
109	421	683	947	1201	1471	1721	1993
113	431	691	953	1213	1481	1723	1997
127	433	701	967	1217	1483	1733	1999
131	439	709	971	1223	1487	1741	
137	443	719	977	1229	1489	1747	
139	449	727	983	1231	1493		
149	457	733	991	1237	1499		
151	461	739	997	1249			
157	463	743					
163	467						
167	479						
173	487						
179	491						
181	499						
191							
193							
197							
199							
211							
223							
227							
229							
233							
239							
241							

Appendix

Even Numbers as the Sum of Two Primes

4 = 2+2
6 = 3+3
8 = 3+5
10 = 3+7; 5+5
12 = 5+7
14 = 3+11; 7+7
16 = 3+13; 5+11
18 = 5+13; 7+11
20 = 3+17; 7+13
22 = 3+19; 5+17; 11+11
24 = 5+19; 7+17; 11+13
26 = 3+23; 7+19; 13+13
28 = 5+23; 11+17
30 = 7+23; 11+19; 13+17
32 = 3+29; 13+19
34 = 3+31; 5+29; 11+23; 17+17
36 = 5+31; 7+29; 13+23; 17+19
38 = 7+31; 19+19
40 = 3+37; 11+29; 17+23
42 = 5+37; 11+31; 13+29; 19+23
44 = 3+41; 7+37; 13+31
46 = 3+43; 5+41; 17+29; 23+23
48 = 5+43; 7+41; 11+37; 17+31; 19+29
50 = 3+47; 7+43; 13+37; 19+31
52 = 5+47; 11+41; 23+29

54 = 7+47; 11+43; 13+41; 17+37; 23+31
56 = 3+53; 13+43; 19+37
58 = 5+53; 11+47; 17+41; 29+29
60 = 7+53; 13+47; 17+43; 19+41; 23+37; 29+31
62 = 3+59; 19+43; 31+31
64 = 3+61; 5+59; 11+53; 17+47; 23+41
66 = 5+61; 7+59; 13+53; 19+47; 23+43; 29+37
68 = 7+61; 31+37
70 = 3+67; 11+59; 17+53; 23+47; 29+41
72 = 5+67; 11+61; 13+59; 19+53; 29+43; 31+41
74 = 3+71; 7+67; 13+61; 31+43; 37+37
76 = 3+73; 5+71; 17+59; 23+53; 29+47
78 = 5+73; 7+71; 11+67; 17+61; 19+59; 31+47; 37+41
80 = 7+73; 13+67; 19+61; 37+43
82 = 3+79; 11+71; 23+59; 29+53; 41+41
84 = 5+79; 11+73; 13+71; 17+67; 23+61; 31+53; 37+47; 41+43
86 = 3+83; 7+79; 13+73; 19+67; 43+43
88 = 5+83; 17+71; 29+59; 41+47
90 = 7+83; 11+79; 17+73; 19+71; 23+67; 29+61; 31+59; 37+53; 43+47
92 = 3+89; 13+79; 19+73; 31+61
94 = 5+89; 11+83; 23+71; 41+53; 47+47
96 = 7+89; 13+83; 17+79; 23+73; 29+67; 37+59; 43+53
98 = 19+79; 31+67; 37+61
100 = 3+97; 11+89; 17+83; 29+71; 41+59; 47+53

102 = 5+97; 13+89; 19+83; 23+79; 29+73; 31+71; 41+61; 43+59
104 = 3+101; 7+97; 31+73; 37+67; 43+61
106 = 3+103; 5+101; 17+89; 23+83; 47+59; 53+53
108 = 5+103; 7+101; 11+97; 19+89; 29+79; 37+71; 41+67; 47+61
110 = 3+107; 7+103; 13+97; 31+79; 37+73; 43+67
112 = 3+109; 5+107; 11+101; 23+89; 29+83; 41+71; 53+59
114 = 5+109; 7+107; 11+103; 13+101; 17+97; 31+83; 41+73; 43+71; 47+67; 53+61
116 = 3+113; 7+109; 13+103; 19+97; 37+79; 43+73
118 = 5+113; 11+107; 17+101; 29+89; 47+71; 59+59
120 = 7+113; 11+109; 13+107; 17+103; 19+101; 23+97; 31+89; 37+83; 41+79; 47+73; 53+67; 59+61
122 = 13+109; 19+103; 43+79; 61+61
124 = 11+113; 17+107; 23+101; 41+83; 53+71
126 = 13+113; 17+109; 19+107; 23+103; 29+97; 37+89; 43+83; 47+79; 53+73; 59+67
128 = 19+109; 31+97; 61+67
130 = 3+127; 17+113; 23+107; 29+101; 41+89; 47+83; 59+71
132 = 5+127; 19+113; 23+109; 29+103; 31+101; 43+89; 53+79; 59+73; 61+71
134 = 3+131; 7+127; 31+103; 37+97; 61+73; 67+67
136 = 5+131; 23+113; 29+107; 47+89; 53+83
138 = 7+131; 11+127; 29+109; 31+107; 37+101; 41+97; 59+79; 67+71
140 = 3+137; 13+127; 31+109; 37+103; 43+97; 61+79; 67+73
142 = 3+139; 5+137; 11+131; 29+113; 41+101; 53+89; 59+83; 71+71
144 = 5+139; 7+137; 13+131; 17+127; 31+113; 37+107; 41+103; 43+101; 47+97; 61+83; 71+73
146 = 7+139; 19+127; 37+109; 43+103; 67+79; 73+73
148 = 11+137; 17+131; 41+107; 47+101; 59+89
150 = 11+139; 13+137; 19+131; 23+127; 37+113; 41+109; 43+107; 47+103; 53+97; 61+89; 67+83; 71+79

Appendix
Odd Numbers as the Difference of Two Squares

$3 = 2^2 - 1^2$
$5 = 3^2 - 2^2$
$7 = 4^2 - 3^2$
$9 = 5^2 - 4^2$
$11 = 6^2 - 5^2$
$13 = 7^2 - 6^2$
$15 = 4^2 - 1^2; \ 8^2 - 7^2$
$17 = 9^2 - 8^2$
$19 = 10^2 - 9^2$
$21 = 5^2 - 2^2; \ 11^2 - 10^2$
$23 = 12^2 - 11^2$
$25 = 13^2 - 12^2$
$27 = 6^2 - 3^2; \ 14^2 - 13^2$
$29 = 15^2 - 14^2$
$31 = 16^2 - 15^2$
$33 = 7^2 - 4^2; \ 17^2 - 16^2$
$35 = 6^2 - 1^2; \ 18^2 - 17^2$
$37 = 19^2 - 18^2$
$39 = 8^2 - 5^2; \ 20^2 - 19^2$
$41 = 21^2 - 20^2$
$43 = 22^2 - 21^2$
$45 = 7^2 - 2^2; \ 9^2 - 6^2; \ 23^2 - 22^2$
$47 = 24^2 - 23^2$
$49 = 25^2 - 24^2$
$51 = 10^2 - 7^2; \ 26^2 - 25^2$
$53 = 27^2 - 26^2$
$55 = 8^2 - 3^2; \ 28^2 - 27^2$
$57 = 11^2 - 8^2; \ 29^2 - 28^2$
$59 = 30^2 - 29^2$
$61 = 31^2 - 30^2$
$63 = 8^2 - 1^2; \ 12^2 - 9^2; \ 32^2 - 31^2$
$65 = 9^2 - 4^2; \ 33^2 - 32^2$
$67 = 34^2 - 33^2$
$69 = 13^2 - 10^2; \ 35^2 - 34^2$
$71 = 36^2 - 35^2$
$73 = 37^2 - 36^2$
$75 = 10^2 - 5^2; \ 14^2 - 11^2; \ 38^2 - 37^2$
$77 = 9^2 - 2^2; \ 39^2 - 38^2$
$79 = 40^2 - 39^2$
$81 = 15^2 - 12^2; \ 41^2 - 40^2$
$83 = 42^2 - 41^2$
$85 = 11^2 - 6^2; \ 43^2 - 42^2$
$87 = 16^2 - 13^2; \ 44^2 - 43^2$
$89 = 45^2 - 44^2$
$91 = 10^2 - 3^2; \ 46^2 - 45^2$
$93 = 17^2 - 14^2; \ 47^2 - 46^2$
$95 = 12^2 - 7^2; \ 48^2 - 47^2$
$97 = 49^2 - 48^2$
$99 = 10^2 - 1^2; \ 18^2 - 15^2; \ 50^2 - 49^2$

$101 = 51^2 - 50^2$
$103 = 52^2 - 51^2$
$105 = 11^2 - 4^2; \ 13^2 - 8^2; \ 19^2 - 16^2; \ 53^2 - 52^2$
$107 = 54^2 - 53^2$
$109 = 55^2 - 54^2$
$111 = 20^2 - 17^2; \ 56^2 - 55^2$
$113 = 57^2 - 56^2$
$115 = 14^2 - 9^2; \ 58^2 - 57^2$
$117 = 11^2 - 2^2; \ 21^2 - 18^2; \ 59^2 - 58^2$
$119 = 12^2 - 5^2; \ 60^2 - 59^2$
$121 = 61^2 - 60^2$
$123 = 22^2 - 19^2; \ 62^2 - 61^2$
$125 = 15^2 - 10^2; \ 63^2 - 62^2$
$127 = 64^2 - 63^2$
$129 = 23^2 - 20^2; \ 65^2 - 64^2$
$131 = 66^2 - 65^2$
$133 = 13^2 - 6^2; \ 67^2 - 66^2$
$135 = 12^2 - 3^2; \ 16^2 - 11^2; \ 24^2 - 21^2; \ 68^2 - 67^2$
$137 = 69^2 - 68^2$
$139 = 70^2 - 69^2$
$141 = 25^2 - 22^2; \ 71^2 - 70^2$
$143 = 12^2 - 1^2; \ 72^2 - 71^2$
$145 = 17^2 - 12^2; \ 73^2 - 72^2$
$147 = 14^2 - 7^2; \ 26^2 - 23^2; \ 74^2 - 73^2$
$149 = 75^2 - 74^2$
$151 = 76^2 - 75^2$
$153 = 13^2 - 4^2; \ 27^2 - 24^2; \ 77^2 - 76^2$
$155 = 18^2 - 13^2; \ 78^2 - 77^2$
$157 = 79^2 - 78^2$
$159 = 28^2 - 25^2; \ 80^2 - 79^2$
$161 = 15^2 - 8^2; \ 81^2 - 80^2$
$163 = 82^2 - 81^2$
$165 = 13^2 - 2^2; \ 19^2 - 14^2; \ 29^2 - 26^2; \ 83^2 - 82^2$
$167 = 84^2 - 83^2$
$169 = 85^2 - 84^2$
$171 = 14^2 - 5^2; \ 30^2 - 27^2; \ 86^2 - 85^2$
$173 = 87^2 - 86^2$
$175 = 16^2 - 9^2; \ 20^2 - 15^2; \ 88^2 - 87^2$
$177 = 31^2 - 28^2; \ 89^2 - 88^2$
$179 = 90^2 - 89^2$
$181 = 91^2 - 90^2$
$183 = 32^2 - 29^2; \ 92^2 - 91^2$
$185 = 21^2 - 16^2; \ 93^2 - 92^2$
$187 = 14^2 - 3^2; \ 94^2 - 93^2$
$189 = 15^2 - 6^2; \ 17^2 - 10^2; \ 33^2 - 30^2; \ 95^2 - 94^2$
$191 = 96^2 - 95^2$
$193 = 97^2 - 96^2$
$195 = 14^2 - 1^2; \ 22^2 - 17^2; \ 34^2 - 31^2; \ 98^2 - 97^2$
$197 = 99^2 - 98^2$
$199 = 100^2 - 99^2$

Appendix

Numbers as the Sum of Two Squares

(Numbers that are missing cannot be expressed as the sum of two squares.)

$2 = 1^2 + 1^2$
$5 = 1^2 + 2^2$
$8 = 2^2 + 2^2$
$10 = 1^2 + 3^2$
$13 = 2^2 + 3^2$
$17 = 1^2 + 4^2$
$18 = 3^2 + 3^2$
$20 = 2^2 + 4^2$
$25 = 3^2 + 4^2$
$26 = 1^2 + 5^2$
$29 = 2^2 + 5^2$
$32 = 4^2 + 4^2$
$34 = 3^2 + 5^2$
$37 = 1^2 + 6^2$
$40 = 2^2 + 6^2$
$41 = 4^2 + 5^2$
$45 = 3^2 + 6^2$
$50 = 1^2 + 7^2; \; 5^2 + 5^2$
$52 = 4^2 + 6^2$
$53 = 2^2 + 7^2$
$58 = 3^2 + 7^2$
$61 = 5^2 + 6^2$
$65 = 1^2 + 8^2; \; 4^2 + 7^2$
$68 = 2^2 + 8^2$
$72 = 6^2 + 6^2$
$73 = 3^2 + 8^2$
$74 = 5^2 + 7^2$
$80 = 4^2 + 8^2$
$82 = 1^2 + 9^2$
$85 = 2^2 + 9^2; \; 6^2 + 7^2$
$89 = 5^2 + 8^2$
$90 = 3^2 + 9^2$
$97 = 4^2 + 9^2$
$98 = 7^2 + 7^2$
$100 = 6^2 + 8^2$
$101 = 1^2 + 10^2$
$104 = 2^2 + 10^2$
$106 = 5^2 + 9^2$
$109 = 3^2 + 10^2$
$113 = 7^2 + 8^2$
$116 = 4^2 + 10^2$
$117 = 6^2 + 9^2$
$122 = 1^2 + 11^2$
$125 = 2^2 + 11^2; \; 5^2 + 10^2$
$128 = 8^2 + 8^2$
$130 = 3^2 + 11^2; \; 7^2 + 9^2$
$136 = 6^2 + 10^2$
$137 = 4^2 + 11^2$
$145 = 1^2 + 12^2; \; 8^2 + 9^2$
$146 = 5^2 + 11^2$

$148 = 2^2 + 12^2$
$149 = 7^2 + 10^2$
$153 = 3^2 + 12^2$
$157 = 6^2 + 11^2$
$160 = 4^2 + 12^2$
$162 = 9^2 + 9^2$
$164 = 8^2 + 10^2$
$169 = 5^2 + 12^2$
$170 = 1^2 + 13^2; \; 7^2 + 11^2$
$173 = 2^2 + 13^2$
$178 = 3^2 + 13^2$
$180 = 6^2 + 12^2$
$181 = 9^2 + 10^2$
$185 = 4^2 + 13^2; \; 8^2 + 11^2$
$193 = 7^2 + 12^2$
$194 = 5^2 + 13^2$
$197 = 1^2 + 14^2$
$200 = 2^2 + 14^2; \; 10^2 + 10^2$
$202 = 9^2 + 11^2$
$205 = 3^2 + 14^2; \; 6^2 + 13^2$
$208 = 8^2 + 12^2$
$212 = 4^2 + 14^2$
$218 = 7^2 + 13^2$
$221 = 5^2 + 14^2; \; 10^2 + 11^2$
$225 = 9^2 + 12^2$
$226 = 1^2 + 15^2$
$229 = 2^2 + 15^2$
$232 = 6^2 + 14^2$
$233 = 8^2 + 13^2$
$234 = 3^2 + 15^2$
$241 = 4^2 + 15^2$
$242 = 11^2 + 11^2$
$244 = 10^2 + 12^2$
$245 = 7^2 + 14^2$
$250 = 5^2 + 15^2; \; 9^2 + 13^2$
$257 = 1^2 + 16^2$
$260 = 2^2 + 16^2; \; 8^2 + 14^2$
$261 = 6^2 + 15^2$
$265 = 3^2 + 16^2; \; 11^2 + 12^2$
$269 = 10^2 + 13^2$
$272 = 4^2 + 16^2$
$274 = 7^2 + 15^2$
$277 = 9^2 + 14^2$
$281 = 5^2 + 16^2$
$288 = 12^2 + 12^2$
$289 = 8^2 + 15^2$
$290 = 1^2 + 17^2; \; 11^2 + 13^2$
$292 = 6^2 + 16^2$
$293 = 2^2 + 17^2$
$296 = 10^2 + 14^2$

$298 = 3^2 + 17^2$
$305 = 4^2 + 17^2; \; 7^2 + 16^2$
$306 = 9^2 + 15^2$
$313 = 12^2 + 13^2$
$314 = 5^2 + 17^2$
$317 = 11^2 + 14^2$
$320 = 8^2 + 16^2$
$325 = 1^2 + 18^2; \; 6^2 + 17^2; \; 10^2 + 15^2$
$328 = 2^2 + 18^2$
$333 = 3^2 + 18^2$
$337 = 9^2 + 16^2$
$338 = 7^2 + 17^2; \; 13^2 + 13^2$
$340 = 4^2 + 18^2; \; 12^2 + 14^2$
$346 = 11^2 + 15^2$
$349 = 5^2 + 18^2$
$353 = 8^2 + 17^2$
$356 = 10^2 + 16^2$
$360 = 6^2 + 18^2$
$362 = 1^2 + 19^2$
$365 = 2^2 + 19^2; \; 13^2 + 14^2$
$369 = 12^2 + 15^2$
$370 = 3^2 + 19^2; \; 9^2 + 17^2$
$373 = 7^2 + 18^2$
$377 = 4^2 + 19^2; \; 11^2 + 16^2$
$386 = 5^2 + 19^2$
$388 = 8^2 + 18^2$
$389 = 10^2 + 17^2$
$392 = 14^2 + 14^2$
$394 = 13^2 + 15^2$
$397 = 6^2 + 19^2$
$400 = 12^2 + 16^2$
$401 = 1^2 + 20^2$
$404 = 2^2 + 20^2$
$405 = 9^2 + 18^2$
$409 = 3^2 + 20^2$
$410 = 7^2 + 19^2; \; 11^2 + 17^2$
$416 = 4^2 + 20^2$
$421 = 14^2 + 15^2$
$424 = 10^2 + 18^2$
$425 = 5^2 + 20^2; \; 8^2 + 19^2; \; 13^2 + 16^2$
$433 = 12^2 + 17^2$
$436 = 6^2 + 20^2$
$442 = 1^2 + 21^2; \; 9^2 + 19^2$

The first number that can be expressed in 4 ways is...
$1105 = 4^2 + 33^2; \; 9^2 + 32^2;$
$\qquad\quad 12^2 + 31^2; \; 23^2 + 24^2$

85